P9-CDG-886

Globalization: A Very Short Introduction

VERY SHORT INTRODUCTIONS are for anyone wanting a stimulating and accessible way into a new subject. They are written by experts, and have been translated into more than 45 different languages.

The series began in 1995, and now covers a wide variety of topics in every discipline. The VSI library now contains over 500 volumes—a Very Short Introduction to everything from Psychology and Philosophy of Science to American History and Relativity—and continues to grow in every subject area.

Very Short Introductions available now:

Available soon:

For more information visit our website

www.oup.com/vsi/

Manfred B. Steger

GLOBALIZATION

A Very Short Introduction

Fourth edition

OXFORD
UNIVERSITY PRESS

OXFORD
UNIVERSITY PRESS

Great Clarendon Street, Oxford, OX2 6DP,
United Kingdom

Oxford University Press is a department of the University of Oxford.
It furthers the University's objective of excellence in research, scholarship,
and education by publishing worldwide. Oxford is a registered trade mark of
Oxford University Press in the UK and in certain other countries

© Manfred B. Steger 2017
First edition published 2003
Second edition published 2009
Third edition published 2013
This edition published 2017

The moral rights of the author have been asserted

Impression: 7

Published in the United States of America by Oxford University Press
198 Madison Avenue, New York, NY 10016, United States of America

British Library Cataloguing in Publication Data
Data available

Library of Congress Control Number: 2016958129

ISBN 978-0-19-877955-1

Printed in Great Britain by
Ashford Colour Press Ltd, Gosport, Hampshire

Links to third party websites are provided by Oxford in good faith and
for information only. Oxford disclaims any responsibility for the materials
contained in any third party website referenced in this work.

Contents

Preface to the fourth edition

It is a gratifying experience to present readers with the fourth
edition of a short book that has been so well received—not only in
the English-speaking world, but, as its translation record shows,
around the globe. The necessary task of updating and expanding
the third edition in light of pressing global problems such as
growing social inequality, the uptick of global terrorism under the
ideological leadership of ISIL, the escalating climate crisis, the
growing refugee streams pouring out of the Middle East and
Africa, and the unexpected US presidential election victory of
national populist Donald Trump has made it difficult to keep
a book on such a complex topic as globalization short and
accessible. This challenge becomes even more formidable in the
case of a *very short* introduction. For this reason, the authors
of the few existing *short* introductions to the subject have
found it sensible to concentrate on only one or two aspects of
globalization—usually the ICT revolution and the intertwined
emergence of the global economic system, its history, structure,
and supposed benefits and shortcomings. While helpful in
explaining the intricacies of new digital devices and social
networking platforms connecting people across borders,
international trade policy, global financial markets, worldwide
flows of goods, services, and labour, transnational corporations,
and the outsourcing of jobs to developing regions, such narrow
accounts often leave the general reader with a limited

understanding of globalization as primarily an economic phenomenon mediated by cutting-edge digital technologies.

While the discussion of such dynamics ought to be a significant part of any comprehensive account of globalization, we can hardly afford to stop there. The transformative powers of globalization reach deeply into *all* aspects of contemporary social life. For this reason, the present volume makes the case that globalization is best thought of as a multidimensional set of objective *and* subjective processes that resists confinement to any single thematic framework. In fact, globalization contains important *cultural* and *ideological* aspects in the form of politically charged meanings, stories, and symbols that define, describe, and analyse that very process. The global media and other social forces behind these competing accounts of globalization seek to endow this concept with norms, values, and understandings that not only legitimize and advance specific power interests, but also shape the personal and collective identities of billions of people. After all, it is mostly the *normative* question of whether globalization ought to be considered a 'good' or a 'bad' thing that has spawned heated debates in classrooms, boardrooms, and on the streets.

Some commentators applaud globalization for its ability to lift millions of people out of poverty and provide instant communication and access to information. Others condemn it as a destructive force bound to annihilate traditional communal values, wreck our planet, and stretch the disparities in people's wellbeing beyond sustainable levels. Paradoxically, the advocates of both perspectives advance sound arguments and cite tons of 'empirical data' to bolster their respective views. Regardless of which position one favours, it is important to maintain a critical stance that pays attention to the power dynamics involved in globalization.

Following this *critical imperative*, this book offers both a descriptive and explanatory account of various dimensions of globalization, including its ideological aspects and normative implications. But my critical approach should not be interpreted as a blanket rejection of globalization itself. After all, one might question the practices of TNCs, yet appreciate the role of regulated markets in facilitating essential material exchanges necessary for human wellbeing. On the whole, I am well disposed toward globalization. I believe that we should take comfort in the fact that the world is becoming a more interdependent place that enhances people's chances to acknowledge their common humanity across arbitrarily drawn political borders and cultural divides. I also welcome the global flow of ideas and goods, as well as the sustainable development of technology, provided that they go hand in hand with greater forms of freedom and equality for *all* people, especially those living in the disadvantaged regions of the global South.

Today, the study of globalization extends beyond any single academic discipline. Yet, its lack of a firm disciplinary home also contains great opportunities. 'Global Studies' has emerged as a popular new field of academic study organized around four major conceptual 'pillars': globalization, transdisciplinarity, space and time, and critical thinking. Hundreds of Global Studies programmes have been established on all continents that invite students to study globalization across traditional disciplinary boundaries in the social sciences, humanities, and even the natural sciences. Large Global Studies programmes like the one at the University of California Santa Barbara have attracted more than a thousand undergraduate majors. Global Studies encourages students to familiarize themselves with vast literatures on related subjects that are usually studied in isolation from each other. The greatest challenge facing the new field lies, therefore, in connecting and synthesizing the various strands of knowledge in a way that does justice to the increasingly fluid and interdependent nature of our fast-changing world.

Let me end this Preface by recording my debts of gratitude. I want to thank my colleagues and students at the University of

Hawai'i-Mānoa and the Royal Melbourne Institute of Technology (RMIT University). Special thanks are due to Paul James, the Director of the Institute for Culture and Society at Western Sydney University, for his steady intellectual encouragement and loyal friendship. I appreciate the engagement of my colleagues from around the world who have channelled much of their enthusiasm for the study of globalization into the development of the Global Studies Consortium, a transcontinental professional organization dedicated to strengthening the new transdisciplinary field. I also want to express my deep appreciation to numerous readers, reviewers, and audiences around the world, who, for nearly two decades, have made insightful comments in response to my public lectures and publications on the subject of globalization. Dr Franz Broswimmer, a dear friend and innovative environmentalist, deserves special recognition for supplying me with valuable information on the ecological aspects of globalization. Andrea Keegan and Jenny Nugee, my editors at Oxford University Press, have been shining examples of professionalism and competence. Finally, I want to thank my wife Perle—as well as the Steger and Besserman families—for their love and support. Many people have contributed to improving the quality of this book; its remaining flaws are my own responsibility.

List of abbreviations

AOL	America Online
APEC	Asian Pacific Economic Cooperation
ASEAN	Association of South East Asian Nations
BCE	Before the Common Era
CE	Common Era
CEO	chief executive officer
CFCs	chlorofluorocarbons
CITES	Convention on International Trade in Endangered Species of Wild Flora and Fauna
CNBC	Cable National Broadcasting Corporation
CNN	Cable News Network
ECB	European Central Bank
EU	European Union
FBI	United States Federal Bureau of Investigation
FIFA	Fédération Internationale de Football Association (International Federation of Association Football)
FTAA	Free Trade Area of the Americas
G8	Group of Eight
G20	Group of Twenty
GATT	General Agreement of Tariffs and Trade
GCC	Global Climate Crisis
GDP	gross domestic product
GFC	Global Financial Crisis

GJM	Global Justice Movement
GNP	gross national product
HIPC	Heavily Indebted Poor Countries Initiative
ICT	information and communications technology
IMF	International Monetary Fund
INGO	international non-governmental organization
IRS	United States Internal Revenue Service
ISIL	Islamic State of Iraq and the Levant
MAI	Multilateral Agreement on Investment
MERCOSUR	Mercado Común del Sur (Southern Common Market)
MSF/DWB	Médecins Sans Frontières/Doctors Without Borders
MTV	Music Television
NAFTA	North American Free Trade Agreement
NATO	North Atlantic Treaty Organization
NGO	non-governmental organization
NOAA	US National and Oceanic and Atmospheric Administration
OECD	Organization for Economic Cooperation and Development
OPEC	Organization of Petroleum Exporting Countries
TNCs	transnational corporations
UEFA	Union of European Football Associations
UN	United Nations
UNCTAD	United Nations Conference on Trade and Development
UNESCO	United Nations Educational, Scientific, and Cultural Organization
UNIPCC	United Nations Intergovernmental Panel on Climate Change
WEF	World Economic Forum
WHO	World Health Organization
WSF	World Social Forum

List of illustrations

List of maps

List of figures

Chapter 1
Globalization: a contested concept

Although the earliest appearance of the term 'globalization' in the English language can be traced back to the 1930s, it was not until more than half a century later that the concept took the world by storm. 'Globalization' emerged as *the* buzzword of the 1990s, because it captured the increasingly interconnected nature of social life on our planet mediated by the ICT revolution and the global integration of markets. Twenty-five years later, globalization has remained a hot topic. Indeed, one can track millions of references to the term in both virtual and printed space.

Unfortunately, however, early bestsellers on the subject—for example, Kenichi Ohmae's *The End of the Nation State* or Thomas Friedman's *The Lexus and the Olive Tree*—left their readers with the simplistic impression of globalization as an unstoppable juggernaut, spreading the logic of capitalism and Western values by eradicating local traditions and national cultures. This influential notion of globalization as a ruthless techno-economic steamroller flattening local, national, and regional scales also appeared as the spectre of 'Americanization' haunting the rest of the world. Such widespread fears or hopes, depending on how one felt about such homogenizing forces, deepened further in the 2000s during the so-called Global War on Terror spearheaded by the global military superpower—the United States. Moreover, the current public debates about the power status of America in the age of Trump and the corresponding rise of the 'BRICS' (Brazil, Russia, India, China, and South Africa) have done little to soften this popular dichotomy casting the West against the 'rest'. As a result, many people still have trouble recognizing globalization for what it is: a complex and uneven dynamic linking the local (and the national and regional) to the global—as well as the West to the East, and the North to the South.

As an illustration of such a more nuanced understanding of globalization as a thickening 'global–local nexus'—or what some Global Studies scholars refer to as *glocalization*—let us consider the world's most popular sports event: the men's Football World Cup. First organized in 1930 by the International Federation of Association Football (FIFA), the event was soon seen as the ultimate national contest pitting country against country in the relentless pursuit of patriotic glory. The World Cup has since been held every four years (except for 1942 and 1946) in host countries located on all continents except Oceania. In fact, this transnational rotation of host countries coupled with the event's name 'World Cup' (instead of 'Nations Cup')—gives us a first indication of why the global should not be rigidly separated from the national. But let us delve more deeply into the matter and consider even more telling facts. Indeed, the 2014 World Cup will shed light on the complex 'glocal' dynamics that define the phenomenon we have come to call 'globalization'.

The global–local nexus and the Brazilian World Cup

The twentieth FIFA World Cup for men's national football was held from 12 June to 13 July 2014 in Brazil. The 32 best national teams from a total of 207 original contestants competed for the coveted Golden Globe Trophy. These included five nations from Africa, four from Asia, thirteen from Europe, four from North and Central America, and six from South America. Sixty-four games were played in twelve Brazilian cities, drawing a live crowd of over five million spectators. More than a million tourists

2

from around the world visited Brazil in June 2014, which reflects an increase of nearly 300 per cent from June 2013. More than 70 per cent of international tourists arrived by air, 27 per cent by road, and the rest came by boat. More than 11 million game ticket applications were received by FIFA but only 3 million could be allocated in advance to the general public (see Figure A).

The global–local dynamics are rather obvious here: national teams playing in Brazilian stadiums in front of a mixture of local, national, and global spectators as well as a virtual global audience

Country	No of tickets allocated to the public (by residency)
Brazil	1,636,294
United States	203,964
Argentina	63,128
Germany	60,991
England	58,690
Columbia	52,509
Australia	40,902
Chile	40,200
France	35,347
Mexico	35,006
Canada	30,026
Japan	22,942
Switzerland	17,880
Netherlands	16,374
Uruguay	16,142
Spain	13,886
Israel	12,443
Ecuador	11,762
Russian Federation	10,858
Italy	10,155

A. Global ticket allocations for the 2014 FIFA World Cup in Brazil.

Source: data taken from 'Global Ticket Allocations for the 2014 FIFA World Cup in Brazil', <http://resources.fifa.com/mm/document/tournament/competition/02/44/29/89/fifaworldcupinnumbers_120714_v7_eng_neutral.pdf>

watching the games on TVs and digital streaming devices. Indeed, the Brazilian World Cup was shown in every single country and territory on Earth. The in-home coverage of the competition reached an audience of over 3.2 billion people—45 per cent of the global population—who watched at least a few minutes of the event. A whopping 695 million people followed at least twenty consecutive minutes of the championship match between victorious Germany and runner-up Argentina.

Money matters related to the World Cup are equally 'glocal' in nature. Brazilian authorities spent about $13 billion to finance the mega-event, including $2 billion for security purposes. Still, the World Cup was a good deal for the host nation. The Brazilian Ministry of Tourism reported that tourism and investment would bring in $13.5 billion within a year and an extra $90 billion in revenue over ten years. The World Cup-related infrastructure projects alone generated 1 million jobs, of which 710,000 became permanent. Over the four-year cycle 2010–14, the games generated $4.8 billion in revenue for FIFA. $2.4 billion was made in TV rights, $1.6 billion in sponsorship revenue, with the most significant contracts going to such powerful TNCs as Adidas, Coca-Cola, Visa, Emirates, McDonalds, Castrol, Sony, Hyundai Motor Group, Johnson & Johnson, and Budweiser. When the glocal mega-event ended on 13 July 2014, FIFA happily pocketed a handsome net profit of $338 million, which pushed the transnational organization's total financial reserves to over $1.5 billion.

The official World Cup match-ball, too, was an impressive example of the glocal dynamics constituting globalization. Supplied by Adidas, a successful TNC headquartered in Germany, the football received the name 'Brazuca' from the majority of over a million Brazilian fans voting in a naming contest via social media. Brazuca means 'our fellow' in Portuguese and is used by Brazilians to describe their national pride in their national way of life. In spite of their apparent local and national identity, however, the Brazucas were manufactured by low-wage workers at the Forward Spots

4

factory in the Pakistani town of Sialkot (replica balls were made in China). Designed to have a more accurate and repeatable flight path, the prototype Brazucas were thoroughly tested in locations covering all sorts of climates and altitudes in ten countries on three continents. These trials took nearly three years and involved 600 international players to make sure that the Brazuca worked for all positions of the game. Finally, the football contains chemical compounds produced in several countries and plastics generated from petroleum imported from the Middle East and Norway. South Korean-built supersized container ships carried the transnationally assembled Brazucas to football fans around the world.

What do Lionel Messi and J. Lo have in common?

But perhaps the most striking illustration of how globalization erupts simultaneously within and across all geographical scales involves two of the most celebrated superstars of the Brazilian World Cup: the Argentinian superstar Lionel Andrés Messi, the tournament's most valuable player, and American singer-entertainer Jennifer Lopez. 'J. Lo' performed the official anthem of the 2014 FIFA World Cup at its opening ceremony together with the Cuban-American rapper Armando Christian Pérez ('Pitbull') and celebrated Brazilian singer-songwriter Claudia Leitte ('Claudhina').

Born in 1987 into a working-class family of Spanish and Italian heritage in Rosario, Argentina, little 'Leo', as Lionel was called, developed a passion for football at a very early age. However, his future as a professional player was threatened when, at the age of 10, he was diagnosed with growth hormone deficiency—a malady that required $1,000 per month in hormone treatments. Unable to pay for the injections in a country collapsing under the strain of the economic crisis of 1999–2001—a topic we will turn to in Chapter 3—the Messi family turned for help to relatives in Catalonia, Spain. They managed to arrange Lionel's transfer to the legendary football club FC Barcelona—also known as 'Barça'—in spite of his unusually young age of 13. In 2001, the entire Messi family relocated to Barcelona and moved into an apartment near the club's legendary stadium, Camp Nou. Although Lionel has remained in Barcelona for his entire football career so far, he has maintained close ties to his hometown of Rosario and even refuses to sell the old family house. Indeed, the global football icon has often referred to himself as an Argentine 'local boy'. At the same time, he has not only contributed to the soccer glory of his adopted Spanish city, but has also accepted the global task of serving as a tireless goodwill UNICEF ambassador, engaged in charitable efforts aimed at helping vulnerable children around the world. Still, Messi's positive image was tarnished when a Barcelona court found him and his father guilty of tax fraud and sentenced them to suspended jail sentences and huge monetary fines.

Messi's career at Barça is the stuff of football legends. Considered by some as the best football player of all time, the Argentine striker has broken all club records, leading his team to seven Spanish 'La Liga' national league championships, four European championship titles, and three Copa del Rey titles so far. Messi is to date the only football player in history to win the FIFA's Ballon d'Or Award for Best Male Football Player in the World five times, four of which he won consecutively 2009–12. He has also won three European Golden Shoe awards. Already the all-time scoring leader in both La Liga (over 300 goals) and a single European Champions League match (five goals), the 28-year-old football wizard scored his 500th career goal on 3 February 2016 in a match that pitted Barça against FC Valencia. In that month, Messi's awesome global popularity was reflected in the staggering number of 81,364,376 'Likes' that graced his Facebook page.

Despite his stellar city club achievements, Lionel Messi's greatest moments to date have come on the global stage in Brazil, where he led his national team to an impressive second place finish (see Illustration 1). This made Argentina the most successful

1. Lionel Messi scoring at the 2014 FIFA World Cup.

South American country of the 2014 World Cup, surpassing the dejected host and football superpower Brazil, which placed a disappointing fourth. Proudly wearing the iconic blue and white-striped number 10 jersey of his nation, Messi dazzled local and global fans alike with his ball-playing skills, speed, elegance, and goal-scoring instincts. Although his team lost the championship match against Germany in heart-breaking fashion in extra time, Messi won the Golden Ball for the best player of the tournament. Indeed, the Argentine striker and many of his fellow footballers performing in Brazilian World Cup stadiums embodied the glocal dynamics of globalization as they played for national teams that entertained local and global audiences while simultaneously retaining the football identity that linked them to their contracted clubs in global cities around the world.

A careful deconstruction of FIFA World Cup entertainer Jennifer Lopez reveals similar glocal dynamics that show why we should not approach globalization as a disconnected phenomenon floating above local and national contexts. Jennifer Lynn Lopez was born in 1969 in New York City to Puerto Rican immigrants. Growing up in the world's most multicultural city, J. Lo began performing as a singer and dancer at the age of 5. As a young woman, she danced in a musical chorus that toured Europe and later acted as a singer, dancer, and choreographer in the Japanese TV show *Synchronicity*. Her breakthrough to stardom came in 1997 in the title role of the biographical musical drama *Selena*. The film featured the life and career of the late Tejano music star who exerted a remarkable transcultural appeal across North and Latin America. Thanks to J. Lo's talent, the movie was a big box office success, grossing $35 million in the USA alone.

With a few exceptions, like the 2003 commercial failure of the romantic movie *Gigli*, J. Lo has been enjoying a stellar career as a singer-actor that includes appearances as a judge in the TV mega-show *American Idol*. In 2012, she released 'On the Floor', one of the best-selling singles of all time. The music channel VH1 ranked Lopez in the top tier on its list of the 'Greatest Pop Culture Icons', and she was honoured by the World Music Awards with the Legend Award for her contribution to the arts. Hailed for her ability to traverse difficult racial boundaries, J. Lo developed a musical style that mixes a number of genres such as Latin pop, dance, R&B, hip hop, rock, funk, house, and salsa. In many ways, both her personal background and her style of music can be characterized as a form of 'hybridization'—the process of mixing different cultural elements and styles. As we will explore in more detail in Chapter 5 of this book, such cultural hybridization processes have been greatly accelerated by globalization.

On 12 June 2014, J. Lo took centre stage at FIFA's World Cup Opening Ceremony at the Arena de São Paulo in São Paulo, Brazil (see Illustration 2). In her flashy green, Lebanese-designed playsuit, the sparsely dressed superstar was joined by fellow artists Pitbull and Claudhina in the performance of 'We Are One (Ole Ola)', a song that reached a top 20 spot on the billboard charts of twenty-seven countries on four continents. This glocal

2. J. Lo, Pitbull, and Claudhina performing *We Are One* (*Ole Ola*) at the 2014 FIFA World Cup Opening Ceremony, São Paulo, Brazil, 12 June 2014.

FIFA World Cup anthem was co-written by the performing trio plus six other artists hailing from three continents: the Colombian Daniel Murcia, the Dane Thomas Troelsen, the Australian Sia Furler, the American Lukasz 'Dr Luke' Gottwald, the Canadian Henry 'Cirkuit' Walter, and Moroccan-Swede Nadir Khayat 'RedOne'. A clear example of today's hybrid, global–local creations of material culture, the commercial success of 'We Are One' owed much to the cross-cultural creativity of these songwriters. Moreover, the song served as a global appeal to humanity to come together 'as one' and tackle the serious global problems of the 21st century. Indeed, such global awareness is especially evident in Pitbull's three successful albums that are appropriately titled: *Global Warming* (2012), *Climate Change* (2016), and, yes, *Globalization* (2014).

So what—in addition to their multilingual facility and their remarkable transnational appeal—do the US Latino pop star performing a globalized World Cup anthem and an Argentine football legend playing for a Spanish city club have in common? They are both the products and catalysts of globalization processes that make more sense when considered as a global–local nexus we call 'glocalization'.

In fact, even the embarrassing corruption scandal that rocked FIFA in the years following the immensely popular Brazilian World Cup reflects the global–local dynamics of globalization as they apply to transnational crime. In 2015, the federal US agencies, the FBI and the IRS, arrested several FIFA officials on suspicion of bribery, wire fraud, racketeering, and money laundering. The investigations related to these arrests and eventual indictments also unearthed collusions between South American, Caribbean, and North American sports marketing executives with strong ties to FIFA. A total of eighteen individuals from fifteen countries were indicted, including nine FIFA officials. When it became clear that such global criminal activities had even tainted the selection processes for several FIFA World Cup sites as well as the 2011 FIFA presidential election, the Attorney General of Switzerland decided to investigate Sepp Blatter, the long-term Swiss FIFA President, for criminal mismanagement. In December 2015, FIFA's Ethics Committee—representing all continental football bodies—banned Blatter and Michel Platini, the Head of UEFA, from all football-related activities for eight years (reduced in 2016 to six years). Although the FIFA corruption scandal sorely tested the confidence of billions of global fans in the virtuousness of their beloved sport, it also serves as a perfect example of the glocal character of globalization as evident in the transnational dynamics of localized criminal actions, and the ensuing global cooperation among national government agencies that tracked down the local culprits.

Our deconstruction of the Brazilian World Cup and the corruption scandal following in its wake has prepared us to tackle the rather demanding task of assembling a working definition of a contested concept that has proven notoriously hard to pin down.

Towards a definition of globalization

'Globalization' has been variously used in both the popular press and academic literature to describe a process, a condition, a system, a force, and an age. Given that these competing labels have very different meanings, their indiscriminate usage is often obscure and invites confusion. For example, a sloppy conflation of process and condition encourages circular definitions that explain little. The often-repeated truism that globalization (the process) leads to more globalization (the condition) does not allow us to draw meaningful analytical distinctions between causes and effects.

Hence, I suggest that we adopt three different but related terms. First, *globality* signifies a *social condition* characterized by tight global economic, political, cultural, and environmental interconnections and flows that make most of the currently existing borders and boundaries irrelevant. Yet, we should not assume that globality is already upon us. Nor does the term suggest a determinate endpoint that precludes any further development. Moreover, we could easily imagine different social manifestations of globality: one might be based primarily on values of individualism, competition, and laissez-faire capitalism, while another might draw on more communal norms and cooperative social systems. These possible alternatives point to the fundamentally *indeterminate character* of full-fledged globality.

Second, let us adopt *global imaginary* to refer to people's growing *consciousness* of thickening globality. Again, as we have seen in our example of the 2014 World Cup, this is not to say that national and local communal frameworks have lost their power to provide people with a meaningful sense of home and identity. But it would be a mistake to close one's eyes to the weakening of the national imaginary, as it has been historically constituted in the 19th and 20th centuries. The intensification of global consciousness destabilizes and unsettles the nation-state framework within which people have imagined their communal existence. As we shall see in Chapter 7, the rising global imaginary is also powerfully reflected in the current transformation of the conventional ideologies and social values that go into the articulation of concrete political agendas and programmes.

Finally, *globalization* is a spatial concept signifying a *set of social processes* that transform our present social condition of conventional nationality into one of globality. As we noted in our deconstruction of the Brazilian World Cup, however, this does not mean that the national or the local are becoming extinct or irrelevant. In fact, the national and local are changing their character and social functions as a result of our movement towards globality. At its core, then, globalization is about shifting forms of human contact. Like 'modernization' and other verbal nouns that end in the suffix '-ization', the term 'globalization' suggests a sort of dynamism best captured by the notion of 'development' or 'unfolding' along discernible patterns. Such unfolding may occur quickly or slowly, but it always corresponds to the idea of change, and, therefore, globalization denotes transformation.

Hence, academics exploring the dynamics of globalization are particularly keen on pursuing research questions related to the theme of social change. How does globalization proceed? What is driving it? Does it have one cause or is there a combination of factors? Is globalization a continuation of modernity or is it a radical break? Does it create new forms of inequality and hierarchy? Notice that the conceptualization of globalization as a dynamic process rather than as a static condition forces global studies scholars to pay close attention to new forms of connectivity and integration. Yet, whenever researchers try to bring their object of enquiry into sharper focus, they also heighten the danger of provoking scholarly disagreements over definitions. Our subject is no exception. One of the reasons why globalization remains a contested concept is because there exists no academic consensus on what kinds of social processes should be prioritized.

To make matters worse, globalization is an uneven process, meaning that people living in various parts of the world are affected very differently by this gigantic transformation of social structures and cultural zones. Hence, the social processes that make up globalization have been analysed and explained by various commentators in different, often contradictory ways. Scholars not only hold different views with regard to proper definitions of globalization, they also disagree on its scale, causation, chronology, impact, trajectories, and policy outcomes. The ancient Buddhist parable of the blind scholars and their encounter with the elephant helps to illustrate the academic controversy over the nature and various dimensions of globalization.

Since the blind scholars did not know what the elephant looked like, they resolved to obtain a mental picture, and thus the knowledge they desired, by touching the animal. Feeling its trunk, one blind man argued that the elephant was like a lively snake. Another man, rubbing along its enormous leg, likened the animal to a rough column of massive proportions. The third person took hold of its tail and insisted that the elephant resembled a large, flexible brush. The fourth man felt its sharp tusks and declared it to be like a great spear. Each of the blind scholars held firmly to his own idea of what constituted an elephant. Since their scholarly reputation was riding on the veracity of their respective findings, the blind men eventually ended up arguing over the true nature of the elephant (see Illustration 3).

The ongoing academic quarrel over which dimension contains the essence of globalization represents a postmodern version of the

3. The globalization scholars and the elephant.

parable of the blind men and the elephant. Even those few remaining scholars who still think of globalization as a singular process clash with each other over which aspect of social life constitutes its primary domain. Many global studies experts argue that economic processes lie at the core of globalization. Others privilege political, cultural, or ideological aspects. Still others point to environmental processes as being the essence of globalization. Like the blind men in the parable, each globalization researcher is partly right by correctly identifying *one* important dimension of the phenomenon in question. However, their collective mistake lies in their dogmatic attempts to reduce such a complex phenomenon as globalization to one or two domains that correspond to their own expertise. Surely, a central task for the new field of global studies must be to devise better ways for gauging the relative importance of each dimension without losing sight of the interdependent whole.

Despite such differences of opinion, it is also possible to detect some thematic overlap in various scholarly attempts to identify the core qualities of globalization processes. Consider, for example, the two influential definitions of globalization shown in Box 1.

These definitions point to four additional qualities or characteristics at the core of globalization. First, it involves both the *creation* of new social networks and the *multiplication* of existing connections that cut across traditional political, economic, cultural, and geographical boundaries. As we have seen in the case of the Brazilian World Cup, today's media combine conventional TV coverage with multiple streaming feeds into digital devices and social networking sites that transcend nationally based services.

The second quality of globalization is reflected in the *expansion* and the *stretching* of social relations, activities, and connections. Today's financial markets reach around the globe, and electronic trading occurs around the clock. Gigantic and virtually identical shopping malls have emerged on all continents, catering to those consumers who can afford commodities from all regions of the world—including products whose various components were manufactured in different countries. This process of social stretching applies to FIFA as well as to other non-governmental organizations, commercial enterprises, social clubs, and countless regional and global institutions and associations: the UN, the EU, the Association of South East Asian Nations, the Organization of African Unity, Doctors Without Borders, the World Social Forum, and Google, to name but a few.

Third, globalization involves the *intensification* and *acceleration* of social exchanges and activities. As the Spanish sociologist Manuel Castells has pointed out, the creation of a global network society has been fuelled by 'communication power', which required a technological revolution powered chiefly by the rapid development of new information and communications technologies. Proceeding at breakneck speed, these innovations are reshaping the social landscape of human life. The World Wide Web relays distant information in real time, and satellites provide consumers with instant pictures of remote events. Sophisticated social networking by means of Facebook, Instagram, and Twitter has become a routine activity for more than two billion people around the globe.

Fourth, as we emphasized in our definition of the global imaginary, globalization processes do not occur merely on an objective, material level but they also involve the subjective plane of human consciousness. Without erasing local and national attachments, the compression of the world into a single place has increasingly made global the frame of reference for human thought and action. Hence, globalization involves both the macro-structures of a 'global community' and the micro-structures of 'global personhood'. It extends deep into the core of the personal self and its dispositions, facilitating the creation of multiple individual and collective identities nurtured by the intensifying relations between the personal and the global.

Having succinctly identified the core qualities of globalization, let us now compress them into a single sentence that yields the following *short* definition of globalization:

Globalization refers to the expansion and intensification of social relations and consciousness across world-time and world-space.

Given the subtitle of our book, however, we ought to do even better. So here is the *very short* definition of globalization:

Globalization is about growing worldwide interconnectivity.

In closing, let us consider an important objection raised by some Global Studies scholars sensitive to historical matters: is globalization really all that different from the centuries-old process of modernization? Some critics have responded to this question in the negative, contending that even a cursory look at history suggests that there is not much that is new about contemporary globalization. Hence, before we explore in some detail the main dimensions of globalization, we should give this argument a fair hearing. After all, a critical investigation of globalization's alleged novelty and its relationship to modernity are closely related to yet another question hotly debated in Global Studies: what does a proper chronology and historical periodization of globalization look like? Let us turn to Chapter 2 to find answers to these questions.

Chapter 2
Globalization in history: is globalization a new phenomenon?

If we asked ordinary persons on the busy streets of global cities like New York, Shanghai, or Sydney about the essence of globalization, their answers would probably involve some reference to growing forms of economic connectivity fuelled by digital technologies. People might point to their mobile devices such as Cloud-connected smart wireless phones like the popular iPhone and tablets like the Kindle Oasis linked to powerful Internet search engines like Google Chrome that sort in a split second through gigantic data sets. Or they might mention accessible video-postings on YouTube; ubiquitous social networking sites like Instagram, Facebook, and Twitter; the rapidly expanding blogosphere, satellite- and computer-connected HDTVs, and Netflix movie streaming; interactive 3-D computer and video games; and the new generation of super-jetliners like the Airbus A380 or Boeing's Dreamliner.

As important as technology is for the intensification of global connectivity, it provides only a partial explanation for the latest wave of globalization since the 1980s. Yet, it would be foolish to deny that these new digital technologies have played a crucial role in the compression of world-time and world-space. The Internet (see Figure B), in particular, has assumed a pivotal function in facilitating globalization through the creation of the World Wide Web that connects billions of individuals, civil society associations,

B. What happens in an Internet minute?

Source: based on information from Excelacom, Inc

and governments. Since most of these technologies have been around for less than three decades, it seems to make sense to agree with those commentators who claim that globalization is, indeed, a relatively new phenomenon.

Still, the definition of globalization we arrived at in Chapter 1 stresses the dynamic nature of the phenomenon. The spatial expansion of social relations and the rise of the global imaginary are gradual processes with deep historical roots. The engineers who developed personal computers and supersonic jet planes stand on the shoulders of earlier innovators who created the steam engine, the cotton gin, the telegraph, the phonograph, the telephone, the typewriter, the internal-combustion engine, and

19

electrical appliances. These products, in turn, owe their existence to much earlier technological inventions such as the telescope, the compass, water wheels, windmills, gunpowder, the printing press, and oceangoing ships. And these inventions were the collective achievement of humans in all regions of the world, not just in one privileged geographic 'centre'. In order to acknowledge the full historical record, we might reach back even further to such momentous technological and social achievements as the production of paper, the development of writing, the invention of the wheel, the domestication of wild plants and animals, the slow outward migration of our common African ancestors, and, finally, the emergence of language at the dawn of human evolution.

Thus, the answer to the question of whether globalization constitutes a new phenomenon depends upon how far we are willing to extend the web of causation that resulted in those recent technologies and social arrangements that most people have come to associate with our buzzword. Some scholars consciously limit the historical scope of globalization to the post-1989 era in order to capture its contemporary uniqueness. Others are willing to extend this timeframe to include the groundbreaking developments of the last two centuries. Still others argue that globalization really represents the continuation and extension of complex processes that began with the emergence of modernity and the capitalist world system in the 1500s. And the remaining researchers refuse to confine globalization to time periods measured in mere decades or centuries. Rather, they suggest that these processes have been unfolding for millennia.

No doubt, each of these contending perspectives contains important insights. As we will see in this book, the advocates of the first approach have marshalled impressive evidence for their view that the dramatic expansion and acceleration of global exchanges since the 1980s represents a big leap in the history of globalization. The proponents of the second view correctly emphasize the tight connection between contemporary forms of globalization and the explosion of technology known as the Industrial Revolution. The representatives of the third perspective rightly point to the significance of the time-space compression that occurred in the 16th century when Eurasia, Africa, and the Americas first became connected by enduring trade routes. Finally, the advocates of the fourth approach advance a rather sensible argument when they insist that any truly comprehensive account of globalization falls short without the incorporation of ancient developments and enduring dynamics into our planetary history.

While my short chronology is necessarily fragmentary and general, it identifies five historical periods that are separated from each other by significant accelerations in the pace of social exchanges as well as a widening of their geographical scope. Thus, we could say that globalization is an ancient process that, over many centuries, has crossed distinct qualitative thresholds. In this context, let me reiterate that my chronology does not necessarily imply a linear unfolding of history, nor does it advocate a conventional Eurocentric perspective of world history. Full of unanticipated surprises, violent twists, sudden punctuations, and dramatic reversals, the history of globalization has involved all major regions and cultures of our planet.

The prehistoric period (10000 BCE–3500 BCE)

Let us begin 12,000 years ago when small bands of hunters and gatherers reached the southern tip of South America. This event marked the end of the long process of settling all five continents that was begun by our hominid African ancestors more than one million years ago. Although some major island groups in the Pacific and the Atlantic were not inhabited until relatively recent times, the truly global dispersion of our species was finally achieved. Completed by South American nomads, the success of this endeavour rested on the migratory achievements of their

Siberian ancestors who had crossed the Bering Strait into North America at least a thousand years earlier.

In this earliest phase of globalization, contact among thousands of hunter and gatherer bands spread all over the world was geographically limited and mostly coincidental. This fleeting mode of social interaction changed dramatically about 10,000 years ago when humans took the crucial step of producing their own food. As a result of several factors, including the natural occurrence of plants and animals suitable for domestication as well as continental differences in area and total population size, only certain regions located on or near the vast Eurasian landmass proved to be ideal for these growing agricultural settlements. These areas were located in the Fertile Crescent, north-central China, North Africa, northwestern India, and New Guinea. Over time, food surpluses achieved by these early farmers and herders led to population increases, the establishment of permanent villages, and the construction of fortified towns.

Roving bands of nomads lost out to settled tribes, chiefdoms, and, ultimately, powerful states based on agricultural food production (see Map 1). The decentralized, egalitarian nature of hunter and gatherer groups was replaced by centralized and highly stratified patriarchal social structures headed by chiefs and priests who were exempted from hard manual labour. Moreover, for the first time in human history, these farming societies were able to support two additional social classes whose members did not participate in food production. One group consisted of full-time craft specialists who directed their creative energies toward the invention of new technologies, such as powerful iron tools, beautiful ornaments made of precious metals, complex irrigation canals, sophisticated pottery and basketry, and monumental building structures. The other group comprised professional bureaucrats and soldiers who would later play a key role in the monopolization of the means of violence in the hands of a few rulers, the precise accounting of food surpluses necessary for the

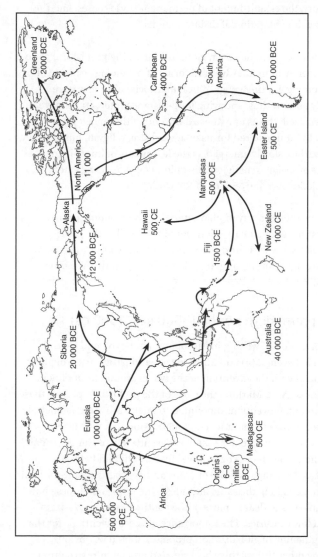

Map 1. Early human migrations.

growth and survival of the centralized state, the acquisition of new territory, the establishment of permanent trade routes, and the systematic exploration of distant regions.

For the most part, however, globalization in the prehistoric period was severely limited. Advanced forms of technology capable of overcoming existing geographical and social obstacles were largely absent; thus, enduring long-distance interactions never materialized. It was only toward the end of this epoch that centrally administered forms of agriculture, religion, bureaucracy, and warfare slowly emerged as the key agents of intensifying modes of social exchange that would involve a growing number of societies in many regions of the world.

Perhaps the best way of characterizing the dynamic of this earliest phase of globalization would be to call it 'the great divergence'—people and social connections stemming from a single origin but moving and diversifying greatly over time and space.

The premodern period (3500 BCE–1500 CE)

The invention of writing in Mesopotamia, Egypt, and central China between 3500 and 2000 BCE (see Illustration 4) roughly coincided with the invention of the wheel around 3000 BCE in Southwest Asia. Marking the close of the prehistoric period, these monumental inventions amounted to one of those technological and social boosts that moved globalization to a new level. Thanks to the auspicious east–west orientation of Eurasia's major continental axis—a geographical feature that had already facilitated the rapid spread of crops and animals suitable for food production along the same latitudes—the diffusion of these new technologies to distant parts of the continent occurred within only a few centuries. The importance of these inventions for the strengthening of globalization processes should be obvious. Among other things, the wheel spurred crucial infrastructural

4. Assyrian clay tablet with cuneiform writing, *c.*1900–1800 BCE.

innovations such as animal-drawn carts and permanent roads that allowed for the faster and more efficient transportation of people and goods. In addition to the spread of ideas and inventions, writing greatly facilitated the coordination of complex social activities and thus encouraged large state formations. Of the sizeable territorial units that arose during this period, only the Andes civilizations of South America managed to grow into the mighty Inca Empire without the benefits of either the wheel or the written word.

The later premodern period was the age of empires. As some states succeeded in establishing permanent rule over other states, the resulting vast territorial accumulations formed the basis of the Egyptian Kingdoms, the Persian Empire, the Macedonian Empire, the American Empires of the Aztecs and the Incas, the Roman Empire, the Indian Empires, the Byzantine Empire, the Islamic Caliphates, the Holy Roman Empire, the African Empires of Ghana, Mali, and Songhay, and the Ottoman Empire. All of these empires fostered the multiplication and extension of long-distance communication and the exchange of culture, technology, commodities, and diseases. The most enduring and technologically advanced of these vast premodern conglomerates was undoubtedly the Chinese Empire. A closer look at its history reveals some of the early dynamics of globalization.

After centuries of warfare among several independent states, the Qin Emperor's armies, in 221 BCE, finally unified large portions of northeast China. For the next 1,700 years, successive dynasties known as the Han, Sui, T'ang, Yuan, and Ming ruled an empire supported by vast bureaucracies that would extend its influence to such distant regions as tropical Southeast Asia, the Mediterranean, India, and East Africa (see Illustration 5). Dazzling artistry and brilliant philosophical achievements stimulated new discoveries in other fields of knowledge such as astronomy, mathematics, and chemistry. The long list of major technological innovations achieved in China during the premodern period includes redesigned ploughshares, hydraulic engineering, gunpowder, the tapping of natural gas, the compass, mechanical clocks, paper, printing, lavishly embroidered silk fabrics, and sophisticated metalworking techniques. The construction of vast irrigation systems consisting of hundreds of small canals enhanced the region's agricultural productivity while at the same time providing for one of the best river transport systems in the world. The codification of law and the fixing of weights, measures, and values of coinage fostered the expansion of trade and markets. The standardization of the size of cart axles and the roads they travelled on allowed Chinese merchants for the first time to make precise calculations as to the desired quantities of imported and exported goods.

The most extensive of these trade routes was the Silk Road. It linked the Chinese and the Roman Empires, with Parthian traders serving as skilled intermediaries. The Silk Road first reached the Italian peninsula in 50 BCE. Even 1,300 years later, a truly multicultural group of Eurasian and African globetrotters—including the famous Moroccan merchant Ibn Battuta and his Venetian counterparts in the Marco Polo family—relied on this great Eurasian land

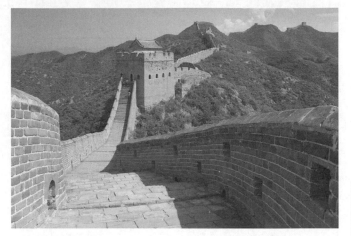

5. The Great Wall of China.

route to reach the splendid imperial court of the Mongol Khans in Beijing.

By the 15th century CE, enormous Chinese fleets consisting of hundreds of 400-foot-long oceangoing ships were crossing the Indian Ocean and establishing short-lived trade outposts on the east coast of Africa. However, a few decades later, the rulers of the Chinese Empire implemented a series of fateful political decisions that halted overseas navigation and mandated a retreat from further technological development. Thus, the rulers cut short their empire's incipient industrial revolution, a development that allowed much smaller and less advanced European states to emerge as the primary historical agents behind the intensification of globalization.

Toward the end of the premodern period, then, the existing global trade network (see Map 2) consisted of several interlocking trade circuits that connected the most populous regions of Eurasia and northeastern Africa. Although both the Australian and the

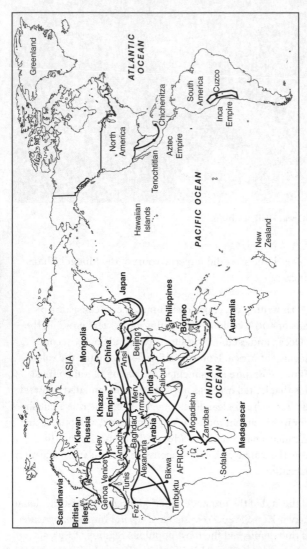

Map 2. Major world trade networks, 1000–1450.

American continents still remained separate from this expanding web of economic, political, and cultural interdependence, the empires of the Aztecs and Incas had also succeeded in developing major trade networks in their own hemisphere.

The existence of these sprawling networks of economic and cultural exchange triggered massive waves of migration, which, in turn, led to further population increase and the rapid growth of urban centres. In the resulting cultural clashes, religions with only local significance were transformed into the major 'world religions' we know today as Judaism, Christianity, Islam, Hinduism, and Buddhism. But higher population density and more intense social interaction over greater distances also facilitated the spread of new infectious diseases like the bubonic plague. The enormous plague epidemic of the mid-14th century, for example, killed up to one-third of the respective populations of China, the Middle East, and Europe. However, these unwelcome by-products of unfolding globalization processes did not reach their most horrific manifestation until the fateful 16th-century collision of the 'old' and 'new' worlds. Although the precise population size of the Americas before contact remains a contentious issue, it is estimated that the deadly germs of European invaders killed an estimated 18–20 million Native Americans—an inconceivable 90–5 per cent of the total indigenous population.

The early modern period (1500–1750)

The term 'modernity' has become associated with the 18th-century European Enlightenment project of developing objective science, achieving a universal form of morality and law, and liberating rational modes of thought and social organization from the perceived irrationalities of myth, religion, and political tyranny. But it is important to acknowledge the existence of multiple forms of modernity that often developed in various parts of the world in resistance to European modernity. The label 'early modern', then, refers to the period between the European Renaissance and the

Enlightenment. During these two centuries, Europe and its social practices emerged as the primary catalyst for globalization after a long period of Asian predominance.

Indeed, having contributed little to technology and other civilizational achievements between about 500 CE and 1000 CE, Europeans north of the Alps greatly benefited from the diffusion of technological innovations originating in the Islamic and Chinese cultural spheres. Despite the weakened political influence of China and the noticeable ecological decline of the Fertile Crescent some 500 years later, European powers failed to penetrate into the interior of Africa and Asia. Instead, they turned their expansionistic desires westward, searching for a new, profitable sea route to India. Their efforts were aided by such innovations as mechanized printing, sophisticated wind and water mills, extensive postal systems, revised maritime technologies, and advanced navigation techniques. Add the enormous impact of the Reformation and the related liberal political idea of limited government, and we have identified the main forces behind the qualitative leap that greatly intensified demographic, cultural, ecological, and economic flows between Europe, Africa, and the Americas.

Of course, the rise of European metropolitan centres and their affiliated merchant classes represented another important factor responsible for strengthening globalization tendencies during the early modern period. Embodying the new values of individualism and unlimited material accumulation, European economic entrepreneurs laid the foundation of what later scholars would call the 'capitalist world system'. However, these fledgling capitalists could not have achieved the global expansion of their commercial enterprises without substantial support from their respective governments. The monarchs of Spain, Portugal, the Netherlands, France, and England all put significant resources into the exploration of new worlds and the construction of new interregional markets that benefited them much more than their exotic 'trading partners'.

By the early 1600s, national joint stock companies like the Dutch and British East India companies were founded for the express purpose of setting up profitable overseas trade posts. As these innovative corporations grew in size and stature, they acquired the power to regulate most intercontinental economic transactions, in the process implementing social institutions and cultural practices that enabled later colonial governments to place these foreign regions under direct political rule (see Illustration 6). Related developments, such as the Atlantic slave trade and forced population transfers within the Americas, resulted in the suffering and death of millions of non-Europeans while greatly benefiting white immigrants and their home countries.

To be sure, religious warfare within Europe also created its share of dislocation and displacement for Caucasian populations. Moreover, as a result of these protracted armed conflicts, military alliances and political arrangements underwent continuous modification. This highlights the crucial role of warfare as a catalyst of globalization. Evolving from the Westphalian states system,

6. The sale of the island of Manhattan in 1626.

the sovereign, territorial nation-state emerged in 18th-century
Europe as the modern container of social life. As the early modern
period drew to a close, interdependencies among nation-states
were intensifying.

The modern period (1750–1980s)

By the late 18th century, Australia and the Pacific islands were
slowly incorporated into the European-dominated network
of political, economic, and cultural exchange. Increasingly
confronted with stories of the 'distant' and images of countless
'Others', Europeans and their descendants on other continents
took it upon themselves to assume the role of the world's guardians
of civilization and morality. In spite of their persistent claims to
universal leadership, however, they remained strangely oblivious
to their racist practices and the appalling conditions of inequality
that existed both within their own societies and between the
global North and South. Fed by a steady stream of materials and
resources that originated mostly in other regions of the world,
Western capitalist enterprises gained in stature. Daring to resist
powerful governmental controls, economic entrepreneurs and
their academic counterparts began to spread a philosophy of
individualism and rational self-interest that glorified the virtues
of an idealized capitalist system supposedly based upon the
providential workings of the free market and its 'invisible hand'.

Written in 1847 by the German political radicals Karl Marx and
Friedrich Engels, a passage taken from their famous *Communist
Manifesto* captures the qualitative shift in social relations that
pushed globalization to a new level in the modern period (see Box 2).

Indeed, the volume of world trade increased dramatically between
1850 and 1914. Guided by the activities of multinational banks,
capital and goods flowed across the borders relatively freely as the
sterling-based gold standard made possible the worldwide
circulation of leading national currencies like the British pound

Box 2 Marx and Engels on globalization

The discovery of America prepared the way for mighty industry and its creation of a truly global market. The latter greatly expanded trade, navigation, and communication by land. These developments, in turn, caused the further expansion of industry. The growth of industry, trade, navigation, and railroads also went hand in hand with the rise of the bourgeoisie and capital which pushed to the background the old social classes of the Middle Ages...Chased around the globe by its burning desire for ever-expanding markets for its products, the bourgeoisie has no choice but settle everywhere; cultivate everywhere; establish connections everywhere...Rapidly improving the instruments of production, the bourgeoisie utilizes the incessantly easing modes of communication to pull all nations into civilization—even the most barbarian ones...In a nutshell, it creates the world in its own image. (Translated by the author)

and the Dutch gilder. Eager to acquire their own independent resource bases, most European nation-states subjected large portions of the global South to direct colonial rule. On the eve of the First World War, merchandise trade measured as a percentage of gross national output totalled almost 12 per cent for the industrialized countries, a level unmatched until the 1970s. Global pricing systems facilitated trade in important commodities like grains, cotton, and various metals. Brand name packaged goods like Coca-Cola drinks, Campbell soups, Singer sewing machines, and Remington typewriters made their first appearance. In order to raise the global visibility of these corporations, international advertising agencies launched the first full-blown trans-border commercial promotion campaigns.

As Marx and Engels noted, however, the rise of the European bourgeoisie and the related intensification of global interconnections would not have been possible without the 19th-century explosion of science and technology. To be sure, the maintenance of these new industrial regimes required new power sources such as electricity and petroleum. The largely unregulated use of these energy sources resulted in the annihilation of countless animal and plant species as well as the toxification of entire regions. On the upside, however, railways, mechanized shipping, and 20th-century intercontinental air transport managed to overcome the last remaining geographical obstacles to the establishment of a genuine global infrastructure, while at the same time lowering transportation costs.

These innovations in transportation were complemented by the swift development of communication technologies. The telegraph and its transatlantic reach after 1866 provided for instant information exchanges between the two hemispheres. Moreover, the telegraph set the stage for the telephone and wireless radio communication, prompting newly emerging communication corporations like AT&T to coin advertising slogans in celebration of a world 'inextricably bound together'. Finally, the 20th-century arrival of mass circulation newspapers and magazines, film, and television further enhanced a growing consciousness of a rapidly shrinking world.

The modern period also witnessed an unprecedented population explosion. Having increased only modestly from about 300 million at the time of the birth of Christ to 760 million in 1750, the world's population reached 4.5 billion in 1980. Enormous waves of migration intensified existing cultural exchanges and transformed traditional social patterns. Popular immigration countries like the United States of America, Canada, and Australia took advantage of this boost in productivity. By the early 20th century, these countries entered the world stage as forces to be reckoned with. At the same time, however, they made significant efforts to control these large migratory flows, in the process inventing novel forms of bureaucratic control and developing new surveillance techniques designed to accumulate more information about nationals while keeping 'undesirables' out.

When the accelerating process of industrialization sharpened existing disparities in wealth and wellbeing beyond bearable limits, many working people in the global North began to organize themselves politically in various labour movements and socialist parties. However, their idealistic calls for international class solidarity went largely unheeded. Instead, ideologies that translated the national imaginary into extreme political programmes captured the imagination of millions of people around the world. There is no question that interstate rivalries intensified at the outset of the 20th century as a result of mass migration, urbanization, colonial competition, and the excessive liberalization of world trade. The ensuing period of extreme nationalism culminated in two devastating world wars, genocides, a long global economic depression, and hostile measures to protect narrowly conceived political communities.

The end of the Second World War saw the explosion of two powerful atomic bombs that killed 200,000 Japanese, most of them civilians. Nothing did more to convince people around the world of the linked fate of geographically and politically separated 'nations'. Indeed, the global imaginary found a horrifying expression in the Cold War acronym 'MAD' (mutually assured destruction). A more positive result was the process of decolonization in the 1950s and 1960s that slowly revived global flows and international exchanges. A new political order of sovereign but interdependent nation-states anchored in the charter of the United Nations raised the prospect of global democratic governance. However, such cosmopolitan hopes quickly faded as the Cold War divided the world for four long decades into two antagonistic spheres: a liberal-capitalist 'First World' dominated by the United States, and an authoritarian-socialist 'Second World' controlled by the Soviet Union. Both blocs sought to establish their political and ideological dominance in the 'Third World'. Indeed, superpower confrontations like the Cuban Missile Crisis raised the spectre of a global conflict capable of destroying virtually all life on our planet.

The contemporary period (from the 1980s)

As we noted at the beginning of this chapter, the dramatic creation, expansion, and acceleration of worldwide interdependencies and global exchanges that have occurred since the 1980s represent yet another quantum leap in the history of globalization. The best way of characterizing this latest globalization wave would be to call it 'the great convergence'—different and widely spaced people and social connections coming together more rapidly than ever before. This dynamic received another boost with the 1991 collapse of the communist Soviet Empire and 'neoliberal' attempts to create an integrated global market. Indeed, the deregulation of national economies combined with the ICT Revolution kicked globalization into a new gear. The unprecedented development of horizontal networks of interactive communication that connected the local and global was made possible through the worldwide diffusion of the Internet, wireless communication, digital media, and online social networking tools.

But how exactly has globalization accelerated in these last three decades? What dimensions of human activity have been most affected by globalization? Is contemporary globalization a 'good' or a 'bad' thing? Throughout this book we will consider possible answers to these crucial questions. In doing so, we will limit the application of the term 'globalization' to the contemporary period while keeping in mind that the forces driving these processes actually can be traced back thousands of years.

Before we embark on this next stage of our globalization journey, let us pause and recall an important point we made in Chapter 1. Globalization is not a single process but a set of processes that operate simultaneously and unevenly on several levels and in various dimensions. We could compare these interactions and interdependencies to an intricate tapestry of overlapping shapes and colours. Yet, just as an apprentice car mechanic must turn off and disassemble the car engine in order to understand its operation, so must the student of globalization apply analytical distinctions in order to make sense of the web of global connectivity. In this book we will identify, explore, and assess patterns of globalization in each of its main domains—economic, political, cultural, ecological, and ideological—while keeping in mind its operation as an interacting whole on all geographical scales. Although we will study the various dimensions of globalization in isolation, we will resist the temptation to reduce globalization to a single 'most important' aspect. Thus will we avoid the blunder that kept the blind men from appreciating the full manifestation of the elephant.

Chapter 3
The economic dimension of globalization

At the beginning of Chapter 2 we noted that new forms of technology configured around the Internet and the social media are among major hallmarks of contemporary globalization. Indeed, technological progress of the magnitude seen in the last three decades is a good indicator for the occurrence of profound social transformations centred on the market. Changes in the way in which people undertake economic production and organize the exchange of commodities represent one obvious aspect of the great transformation of our age. Economic globalization refers to the intensification and stretching of economic connections across the globe. Gigantic flows of capital mediated by digital technology and standardized means of transportation have stimulated trade in goods and services. Extending their reach around the world, markets have migrated to cyberspace and integrated local, national, and regional economies. Huge transnational corporations (TNCs), powerful international economic institutions, and gigantic regional business and trade networks like Asian Pacific Economic Cooperation (APEC) or the European Union (EU) have emerged as the major building blocks of the 21st century's global economic order.

The emergence of the global economic order

Contemporary economic globalization can be traced back to the gradual emergence of a new international economic order assembled at an economic conference held towards the end of the Second World War in the sleepy New England town of Bretton Woods (see Illustration 7). Under the leadership of the United States and Great Britain, the major economic powers of the global North reversed their protectionist policies of the interwar period (1918–39). In addition to arriving at a firm commitment to expand international trade, the participants of the conference also agreed to establish binding rules on international economic activities. Moreover, they resolved to create a more stable monetary exchange system in which the value of each country's currency was pegged to a fixed gold value of the US dollar. Within these prescribed limits, however, individual nations were free to control the permeability of their borders. This allowed national governments to set their own political and economic agendas.

7. The 1944 Bretton Woods Conference.

Bretton Woods also set the institutional foundations for the establishment of three new international economic organizations. The International Monetary Fund (IMF) was created to administer the international monetary system. The International Bank for Reconstruction and Development, later known as the World Bank, was initially designed to provide loans for Europe's postwar reconstruction. During the 1950s, however, its purpose was expanded to fund various industrial projects in developing countries around the world. Finally, the General Agreement on Tariffs and Trade (GATT) was established in 1947 as a global trade organization charged with fashioning and enforcing multilateral trade agreements. In 1995, the World Trade Organization (WTO) was founded as the successor organization to GATT. By the turn of the century, the WTO had become the focal point of intense public controversy over the design and the effects of economic globalization.

In operation for almost three decades, the Bretton Woods regime contributed greatly to the establishment of what some observers have called the 'golden age of controlled capitalism'. Even the most conservative political parties in Europe and the United States embraced some version of state interventionism proposed by British economist John Maynard Keynes, one of the chief architects of the Bretton Woods system. Existing mechanisms of state control over international capital movements made possible full employment and the expansion of the welfare state. Rising wages and increased social services secured in the wealthy countries of the global North a temporary class compromise. In the early 1970s, however, the Bretton Woods system collapsed when President Richard Nixon abandoned the gold-based fixed rate system in response to profound political changes in the world that were undermining the economic competitiveness of US-based industries. The decade was characterized by global economic instability in the form of high inflation, low economic growth, high unemployment, public sector deficits, and two unprecedented energy crises due to the Organization of Petroleum Exporting Countries (OPEC)'s ability to control a large part of the world's oil supply. Political forces in the global North most closely identified with the model of controlled capitalism suffered a series of spectacular election defeats at the hands of conservative political parties that advocated what came to be called a 'neoliberal' approach to economic and social policy.

In the 1980s, British Prime Minister Margaret Thatcher and US President Ronald Reagan emerged as the co-leaders of the 'neoliberal' revolution against Keynesianism (see Box 3). In the same decade, pro-business elites in the USA and Japan consciously linked the novel term 'globalization' to a political agenda aiming at the 'liberation' of state-regulated economies around the world. This budding neoliberal economic order received further legitimization with the 1989–91 collapse of communism in the Soviet bloc.

Box 3 Neoliberalism

Neoliberalism is rooted in the classical liberal ideals of Adam Smith (1723–90) and David Ricardo (1772–1823), both of whom viewed the market as a self-regulating mechanism tending toward equilibrium of supply and demand, thus securing the most efficient allocation of resources. These British philosophers considered that any constraint on free competition would interfere with the natural efficiency of market mechanisms, inevitably leading to social stagnation, political corruption, and the creation of unresponsive state bureaucracies. They also advocated the elimination of tariffs on imports and other barriers to trade and capital flows between nations. British sociologist Herbert Spencer (1820–1903) added to this doctrine a twist of social Darwinism by arguing that free market economies constitute the most civilized form of human competition in which the 'fittest' would naturally rise to the top.

Since then, the three most significant developments related to economic globalization have been the internationalization of trade and finance, the increasing power of transnational corporations and large investment banks, and the enhanced role of international economic institutions like the IMF, the World Bank, and the WTO. But there have also been major global economic setbacks like the Great Recession of 2008–10 or the more recent financial volatility in China and the economic crisis in Brazil intensified by the political instability created in the wake of the 2016 impeachment of President Dilma Rouseff. Let us briefly examine these important dynamics of economic globalization.

The internationalization of trade and finance

Many people associate economic globalization with the controversial issue of free trade. After all, the total value of world trade exploded from $57 billion in 1947 to an astonishing $18.5 trillion in 2015. In that year, China, the world's leading manufacturer, was responsible for 12.7 per cent of global merchandise exports whereas the USA, the world's most voracious consumer, accounted for 12.9 per cent of global merchandise imports.

Indeed, the public debate over the alleged benefits and drawbacks of free trade rages at a feverish pitch as wealthy Northern countries and regional trading blocs have increased their efforts to establish a single global market through far-reaching trade-liberalization agreements. While admitting that these neoliberal sets of trade rules often override national legislation, free trade proponents have nonetheless assured the public that the elimination or reduction of existing trade barriers among nations will increase global wealth and enhance consumer choice. The ultimate benefit of integrated markets, they argue, would be secure peaceful international relations and technological innovation for the benefit of all (see Box 4).

Box 4 Concrete neoliberal measures

1. Privatization of public enterprises.
2. Deregulation of the economy.
3. Liberalization of trade and industry.
4. Massive tax cuts.
5. 'Monetarist' measures to keep inflation in check, even at the risk of increasing unemployment.
6. Strict control on organized labour.
7. The reduction of public expenditures, particularly social spending.
8. The down-sizing of government.
9. The expansion of international markets.
10. The removal of controls on global financial flows.

Indeed, there is evidence that some national economies have increased their productivity as a result of free trade. Millions of people have been lifted out of poverty in developing countries such as China, India, or Indonesia. As the 2015 United Nations' Millennium Goal Report shows, the percentage of people living in extreme poverty (on less than $1.25 a day) in the developing world fell from nearly 50 per cent in 1990 to 14 per cent in 2015. Moreover, there are some clear material benefits that accrue to societies through specialization, competition, and the spread of technology. Still, there are still over 700 million people in the world living in extreme poverty. Moreover, as we will discuss in Chapter 8, inequalities in income and wealth have increased within and across nations. Finally, it is less clear whether the profits resulting from free trade have been distributed fairly within and among various populations.

The internationalization of trade has gone hand in hand with the liberalization of financial transactions. Its key components include the deregulation of interest rates, the removal of credit controls, the privatization of government-owned banks and financial institutions, and the explosive growth of investment banking. Globalization of financial trading allows for increased mobility among different segments of the financial industry, with fewer restrictions and greater investment opportunities. Cutting-edge satellite systems and fibre-optic cables provided the nervous system of Internet-based technologies that further accelerated the liberalization of financial transactions (see Figure C). As captured by the snazzy title of Bill Gates's best-selling book, many people conducted *business@the-speed-of-thought*. Millions of individual investors utilized global electronic investment networks not only to place their orders at the world's leading stock exchanges, but also to receive valuable information about relevant economic and political developments (see Illustration 8).

But a large part of the money involved in this 'financialization' of global capitalism that swept the first decade of the new century had little to do with supplying capital for such productive investments as putting together machines or organizing raw materials and employees to produce saleable commodities. Most

8. The New York Stock Exchange.

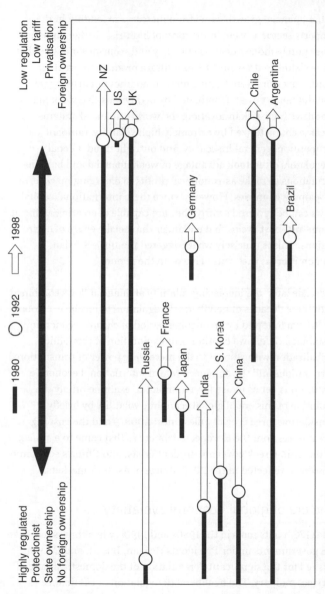

C. The advance of deregulation and liberalization, 1980–1998.

Source: © Vincent Cable, 1999, *Globalization and Global Governance* (The Royal Institute of International Affairs, 1999), used by permission of Bloomsbury Publishing Plc

of the financial growth came from increases in lending in the property sector as well, in the form of high-risk 'hedge funds' and other purely money-dealing currency and securities markets that trade claims to draw profits from future production. In other words, investors were betting on commodities or currency rates that did not yet exist. Dominated by highly sensitive stock markets that drive high-risk innovation, the world's financial systems became characterized by extremely high volatility, rampant competition, general insecurity, and outright fraud. Global speculators often took advantage of weak financial and banking regulations to make astronomical profits in emerging markets of developing countries. However, since these international capital flows can be reversed swiftly, they are capable of creating artificial boom-and-bust cycles that endanger the social welfare of entire regions. This is precisely what triggered the 1997–8 Asian economic crisis that caused havoc in the region.

A decade later, the increasing volatility of financial flows combined with three decades of neoliberal deregulation to produce a global meltdown followed by an ongoing period of chronic economic instability. Before we continue our exploration of economic globalization with respect to the increasing power of transnational corporations and the enhanced role of international economic institutions, let us pause for a moment to examine briefly the evolution of this era of global economic volatility by briefly considering three crucial milestones: 2008/9 and the ensuing Great Recession; the European debt crises that came to a climax in the 2015 Greek government debt crisis; and China's economic slowdown reflected in the 2016 plunge of its stock markets.

The era of global economic volatility

The GFC has its roots in the 1980s and 1990s, when three successive US governments under Presidents Reagan, Bush I, and Clinton pushed for the significant deregulation of the domestic financial services industry. The neoliberal deregulation of US finance capital resulted in a frenzy of mergers that gave birth to huge financial-services conglomerates eager to plunge into securities ventures in areas that were not necessarily part of their underlying business. Derivatives, financial futures, credit default swaps, and other esoteric financial instruments became extremely popular when new computer-based mathematical models suggested more secure ways of managing the risk involved in buying an asset in the future at a price agreed to in the present. Relying far less on savings deposits, financial institutions borrowed from each other and sold these loans as securities, thus passing the risk on to investors in these securities. Other 'innovative' financial instruments such as 'hedge funds' leveraged with borrowed funds fuelled a variety of speculative activities. Billions of investment dollars flowed into complex 'residential mortgage-backed securities' that promised investors up to a 25 per cent return on equity.

Assured by monetarist policies aimed at keeping interest rates low and credit flowing, investment banks eventually expanded their search for capital by buying risky 'subprime' loans from mortgage brokers who, lured by the promise of big commissions, were accepting applications for housing mortgages with little or no down payment and without credit checks. Increasingly popular in the United States, most of these loans were adjustable-rate mortgages tied to fluctuations of short-term interest rates. Investment banks snapped up these high-risk loans knowing that they could resell these assets—and thus the risk involved—by bundling them into composite securities no longer subject to government regulation. Indeed, one of the most complex of these 'innovative' instruments of securitization—so-called 'collateralized debt obligations'—often hid the problematic loans by bundling them together with lower-risk assets and reselling them to unsuspecting investors. Moreover, they were backed by positive credit ratings reports issued by credit ratings giants like Standard and Poor's and Moody's. The high yields flowing from these new securities funds attracted more and more investors around the world, thus rapidly globalizing more than US$1 trillion worth of what came to be known as 'toxic assets'.

In mid-2007, however, the financial steamroller finally ran out of fuel when seriously overvalued American real estate began to drop and foreclosures shot up dramatically. Some of the largest and most venerable financial institutions, insurance companies, and government-sponsored underwriters of mortgages such as Lehman Brothers, Bear Stearns, Merrill Lynch, Goldman Sachs, AIG, Citicorp, J. P. Morgan Chase, IndyMac Bank, Morgan Stanley, Fannie Mae, and Freddie Mac—to name but a few—either declared bankruptcy or had to be bailed out by the US taxpayer. Ultimately, both the conservative Bush II and the liberal Obama administrations championed spending hundreds of billions of dollars on distressed mortgage securities in return for a government share in the businesses involved. Britain and most other industrialized countries followed suit with their own multi-billion dollar bailout packages, hoping that such massive injections of capital into ailing financial markets would help prop up financial institutions deemed 'too big to fail'. But one of the major consequences of the failing financial system was that banks trying to rebuild their capital base could hardly afford to keep lending large amounts of money (see Box 5). The flow of global credit froze to a trickle and businesses and individuals who relied on credit

Box 5 The Global Financial Crisis

When reading about the GFC, huge numbers are splashed around very liberally. In spite of their similar spellings, million, billion, and trillion represent radically different orders of magnitude. Consider this hypothetical situation: if you spent US$1 every second, you would spend US$1 million in about twelve days. At the same rate, it would take you approximately thirty-two years to spend US$1 billion. Taking this to the next level, US$1 trillion would take you 31,546 years to spend!

found it much more difficult to obtain. This credit shortage, in turn, impacted the profitability of many businesses, forcing them to cut back production and lay off workers. Industrial output declined, unemployment shot up, as the world's stock markets dropped dramatically.

By 2009, the GFC had turned into the Great Recession: 14.3 trillion dollars, or 33 per cent of the value of the world's companies, had been wiped out. The developing world was especially hard hit with a financial shortfall of $700 billion by the end of 2010. The leaders of the group of the world's twenty largest economies (G20) met repeatedly in the early 2010s to devise a common strategy to combat a global depression (see Map 3). Although most countries were slowly pulling out of what came to be known as the 'Great Recession', economic growth in many parts of the world remained anaemic and unemployment numbers came down only very slowly.

Soon it became clear that the GFC and its ensuing Great Recession had spawned a severe sovereign debt crisis and a banking crisis, especially in the European Union. This rapidly escalating financial turmoil in the Eurozone not only threatened the fragile recovery of the global economy but almost bankrupted the 'birthplace of Western civilization'—Greece. What came to be known as the 'Greek debt crisis' began in 2009 and 2010—in the wake of the GFC—when the Greek government announced that it had understated its national budget deficits for years and was running out of funds. Shut out from borrowing in global financial markets, the IMF and ECB were forced to put together two gigantic bailout packages totalling $275 billion in order to avoid the country's financial collapse. But the EU lenders imposed harsh austerity terms in exchange for the loan, which caused further economic hardship and failed to restore economic stability. Greece's economy shrank by a quarter and the national unemployed rate shot up to 25 per cent. This disastrous economic development exacerbated people's resentment of

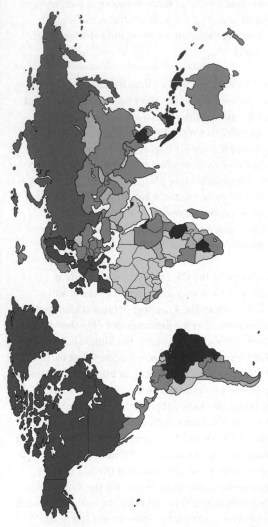

(2007–2009) WORLD FINANCIAL CRISIS

Countries in official recession (two consecutive quarters)

Countries in unofficial recession (one quarter)

Countries with economic slowdown of more than 1.0%

(Between 2007 and 2008, as estimates of December 2008 by the International Monetary Fund)

Countries with economic slowdown of more than 0.5%

Countries with economic slowdown of more than 0.1%

Countries with economic acceleration

Map 3. Countries falling into recession as a result of the Global Financial Crisis, 2007–2009.

the neoliberal policies of austerity and sharpened the country's political polarization.

In 2015, the left-leaning Syriza Party scored a surprising election victory, which made its 41-year-old charismatic leader Alexis Tsipras Greece's new Prime Minister. Assisted by his flamboyant Finance Minister Yanis Varoufakis, Tsipras negotiated a short extension of the loan packages only to face an ultimatum from the Germany-led EU lenders to implement even further austerity measures. Tsipras refused and called for a national referendum on the acceptance of these draconic conditions. The defeat of the so-called 'bailout referendum' by 61 per cent of the popular vote was followed by weeks of frantic negotiations between Tsipras and the other EU leaders. Finally, the creditors offered an even larger multi-billion loan over three years with similar austerity conditions attached (see Figure D). Taking advantage of the defiant popular mood, Tsipras resigned and called for new elections. His gamble paid off when Syriza won a resounding victory on 20 September 2015.

Less than two months later, however, Tsipras was forced to bow to growing popular fears that the dire economic situation in the country would become even worse without the EU bailout package. After a heated debate, the Greek parliament approved of the debt relief measure and promised to implement its highly contentious conditions that included tax increases for farmers and major cuts in the public pension system. But it remains to be seen whether the EU's third bailout package will finally put Greece on a path toward economic recovery. Early signs have not been promising, as the country had to endure a general strike led by outraged farmers in early 2016 that contributed to a precipitous drop of the Athens Stock Exchange.

But Greece was only one among numerous nations that experienced major market declines in this latest round of global economic instability and volatility. The most surprising

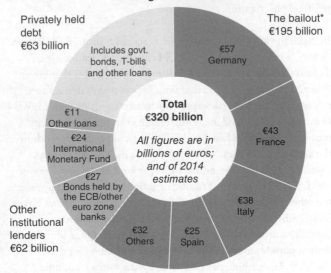

Greek government debt

Privately held debt
€63 billion

Includes govt. bonds, T-bills and other loans

The bailout*
€195 billion

€57 Germany

€11 Other loans

€24 International Monetary Fund

€27 Bonds held by the ECB/other euro zone banks

Other institutional lenders
€62 billion

€43 France

€38 Italy

€32 Others

€25 Spain

Total €320 billion

All figures are in billions of euros; and of 2014 estimates

*European countries lent to Greece through two newly created institutions – €53 billion through the Bilateral Loan Facility and €142 billion through the European Financial Stability Facility. These are in addition to each country's contribution to the IMF.

D. Greek National Debt: who are the creditors?

Source: taken from <http://economydecoded.com/2015/07/how-greece-failed/> with permission. *Sources*: Deutsche Bank, IMF, Reuters, Bloomberg

development occurred in the People's Republic of China—a country many observers consider the bastion of economic health accounting for almost 18 per cent of world economic activity—when its stock markets went into free-fall. In early January 2016, the Shanghai Composite and the Shenzhen Composite lost 5.3 per cent and 6.6 per cent, respectively, in less than a week. The turmoil in the Chinese markets caused equally sharp declines in stock exchanges around the world. After years of historic growth rates of 7 to 9 per cent, China's economy was giving way to less spectacular GDP increases of 3 per cent per year. The major reason behind the country's economic woes was its cooling industrial sector—especially weaknesses of its housing and construction markets as well as its

Globalization

slowing exports. The ripple effects were felt around the world in the form of currency devaluations in South Africa, sharp declines of commodity markets in Brazil and Australia, and disruptions of integrated supply chains in Japan and Korea. But perhaps the most significant impact of the Chinese economic slowdown concerned global oil prices, which fell to the low $30s per barrel in early 2016. As a result, major oil producers such as Russia, Venezuela, and Saudi Arabia took massive hits from the collapse in oil prices. In short, the era of global economic volatility that started with the GFC showed no signs of abating any time soon. In fact, it reached a new climax in June 2016 when 52 per cent of the UK voters opted in favour of the 'leave' option in the 'Brexit' European membership referendum. While the full consequences of the United Kingdom's exit from the European Union will remain unclear for some years, it is a safe bet to expect a continuation of economic volatility in the world.

The power of transnational corporations

Let us now return to our two final topics related to economic globalization: the growing power of TNCs and the enhanced role of international economic institutions. Contemporary versions of the early modern commercial enterprises we discussed in Chapter 2, TNCs are powerful enterprises comprising the parent company and subsidiary units in more than one country, which all operate under a coherent system of decision-making and a common strategy. Their numbers skyrocketed from 7,000 in 1970 to over 100,000 in 2015. Enterprises like General Motors, Wal-Mart, Exxon-Mobil, Mitsubishi, and Siemens belong to the 200 largest TNCs, which account for over half of the world's industrial output. None of these corporations maintains headquarters outside North America, Mexico, Europe, China, Japan, and South Korea. This geographical concentration reflects existing asymmetrical power relations between the North and the South.

Rivalling nation-states in their economic power, these corporations control much of the world's investment capital, technology, and access to international markets. In order to maintain their prominent positions in the global marketplace, TNCs frequently merge with other corporations. In 2015, these corporations spent over 4.7 trillion globally buying one another. Some of these recent mergers include the US$164 billion marriage of the world's largest Internet provider, AOL, with entertainment giant Time-Warner in 2001; the 2013 purchase of Vodafone's Verizon Wireless Inc. by Verizon Communications for $130 billion; and the 2015 'beer merger' uniting Anheuser-Busch InBev with SABMiller for the proud amount of $105 billion.

TNCs have consolidated their global operations in an increasingly deregulated global labour market. The availability of cheap labour, resources, and favourable production conditions in the global South has enhanced corporate mobility and profitability. Accounting for over 70 per cent of world trade, TNCs have boosted their foreign direct investments by approximately 15 per cent annually. As the 2015 UNCTAD *World Investment Report* shows, global foreign direct investment (FDI) undertaken by the 100 largest multinational enterprises is expected to amount to world FDI inflows of $1.7 trillion. Moreover, their ability to disperse manufacturing processes into many discrete phases carried out in many different locations around the world reflects the changing nature of global production. Such transnational production networks allow TNCs like Wal-Mart, General Motors, and Volkswagen to produce, distribute, and market their products on a global scale.

No doubt, the growing power of TNCs has profoundly altered the structure and functioning of the international economy. These giant firms and their global strategies have become major determinants of trade flows, the location of industries, and other economic activities around the world.

A groundbreaking study published in 2011 analysed the relationships between 43,060 large TNCs in terms of share ownerships linking them. The findings revealed that a relatively

Corporation	Industry/ Headquarters	Market value (in US$ billion)	Country (global GDP rank)	GDP (in US$ billion)
1. Apple	Computer hardware	725	Turkey (18)	722
2. Exxon Mobil	Oil and gas operations	357	Austria (30)	373
3. Berkshire Hathaway	Investment services, USA	356	United Arab Emirates (31)	339
4. Google	Computing services, USA	346	South Africa (32)	317
5. Microsoft	Computing software & programming, USA	334	Malaysia (33)	313
6. PetroChina	Oil & gas operations	330	Hong Kong (34)	308
7. Wells Fargo	Banking & finance, USA	280	Colombia (39)	274
8. Johnson & Johnson	Medical equipment & supplies, USA	279.7	Pakistan (40)	271
9. Industrial & Commercial Bank of China	Banking & finance, China	275	Chile (41)	240
10. Novartis	Pharmaceuticals, Switzerland	268	Finland (42)	231

E. Transnational corporations versus countries: a comparison.

Sources: created using data taken from Statista, 2015: <https://www.statista.com/statistics/263264/top- companies-in-the-world-by-market-value/>; Knoema World GDP Rankings 2015, p. 10: <https://knoema.com/nwnfkne/world-gdp-ranking-2015-data-and-charts>; Forbes Global 2000: <http://www.forbes.com/sites/liyanchen/2015/05/06/the-worlds-largest-companies/#4cc16a74fe50>

small core of 1,318 corporations appeared to own collectively through their shares the majority of the world's large blue chip and manufacturing firms. In fact, an even smaller number of these TNCS—147 super-connected corporations to be exact—controlled 40 per cent of the total wealth in the network. Most of them were financial institutions like Barclays Bank, which topped the list. Ironically, it was this very bank that found itself at the centre of a huge scandal that rocked the financial world in July 2012 when it was revealed that Barclays and fifteen other major banks had rigged the world's most important global interest rate for years.

No doubt, over the last decades, TNCs have become extremely important global economic players (see Figure E). The 2015 Forbes Global 2000 list reveals that the largest 2,000 TNCs were headquartered in sixty countries and accounted for combined revenues of US$39 trillion, profits of $3 trillion, with assets worth $162 trillion, and a market value of $48 trillion. Thus, TNCs not only influence the economic, political, and social welfare of billions of individuals, but they also rival entire nations in their economic power. Indeed, in 2015, the ten largest TNCs in the world—as measured by market value—compared favourably to the size of some top-50 national economies.

The enhanced role of international economic institutions

The three international economic institutions most frequently mentioned in the context of economic globalization are the IMF, the World Bank, and the WTO. These three institutions enjoy the privileged position of making and enforcing the rules of a global economy that is sustained by significant power differentials between the global North and South. Since we will discuss the WTO in some detail in Chapter 8, let us focus here on the other two institutions. As pointed out, the IMF and the World Bank emerged from the Bretton Woods system. During the Cold War, their important function of providing loans for developing countries became connected to the West's political objective of containing communism. Starting in the 1970s, and especially after the fall of the Soviet Union, the economic agenda of the IMF and the World Bank largely supported neoliberal interests to integrate and deregulate markets around the world (see Box 6).

In return for supplying much-needed loans to developing countries, the IMF and the World Bank demand from their creditor nations

Box 6 Nokia's role in the Finnish economy

Named after a small town in southwest Finland, Nokia Corporation rose from modest beginnings in 1871 to become the world's largest TNC engaged in the manufacturing of mobile phones and converging Internet industries. In 1998, Nokia sold a record 41 million cellular phones worldwide. At the turn of the century, its products connected more than a billion people in an invisible web around the globe. The engine of Finland's economy, Nokia employed 22,000 Finns—not counting the 20,000 domestic employees who worked for companies that depended on Nokia contracts. The corporation represented two-thirds of the stock market's value and one-fifth of the nation's total export. However, Nokia's gift to Finland—the distinction of being the most interconnected nation in the world—came at the price of economic dependency. The corporation produced a large part of Finland's tax revenue, and its annual sales almost equalled the entire national budget. Yet, when Nokia's growth rate slowed in the late 2000s in the wake of the GFC—10,000 employees were let go in 2012 and some Finnish factories shut down—company executives successfully pressured the Finnish government to reduce its corporate tax rates. Many Finnish citizens complained that such influence wielded by relatively few Nokia managers translated into tax concessions that adversely affected the country's generous and egalitarian welfare system. After further economic setbacks that translated into more layoffs, Nokia sold its mobile phone business to Microsoft in 2013. However, the tax concessions it had received from the Finnish government bought the company the time it needed to design and implement a new business plan focused on network equipment and innovative wireless technology. The success of this strategy was reflected in Nokia's subsequent US $20 billion acquisition of the French telecommunications company Alcatel-Lucent. By 2016, its workforce had rebounded to over 60,000 employees across 120 countries and it had amassed an annual global profit of US $4.2 billion.

the implementation of so-called 'structural adjustment programmes'. Unleashed on developing countries in the 1990s, this set of neoliberal policies is often referred to as the 'Washington Consensus'. It was devised and codified by John Williamson, who was an IMF adviser in the 1970s. The various sections of the programme were mainly directed at countries with large foreign debts remaining from the 1970s and 1980s. The official purpose of the document was to reform the internal economic mechanisms of debtor countries in the developing world so that they would be in a better position to repay the debts they had incurred. In practice, however, the terms of the programme spelled out a new form of colonialism. The ten points of the Washington Consensus, as defined by Williamson, required governments to implement the following structural adjustments in order to qualify for loans:

1. A guarantee of fiscal discipline, and a curb to budget deficits.
2. A reduction of public expenditure, particularly in the military and public administration.
3. Tax reform, aiming at the creation of a system with a broad base and with effective enforcement.
4. Financial liberalization, with interest rates determined by the market.
5. Competitive exchange rates, to assist export-led growth.
6. Trade liberalization, coupled with the abolition of import licensing and a reduction of tariffs.
7. Promotion of foreign direct investment.
8. Privatization of state enterprises, leading to efficient management and improved performance.
9. Deregulation of the economy.
10. Protection of property rights.

It is no coincidence that this programme is called the 'Washington Consensus', for, from the outset, the United States has been the dominant power in the IMF and the World Bank.

Unfortunately, however, large portions of the 'development loans' granted by these institutions have either been pocketed by authoritarian political leaders in the global South or have enriched local businesses and the Northern corporations they usually serve. Sometimes, exorbitant sums are spent on ill-considered construction projects. Most importantly, however, structural adjustment programmes rarely produce the desired result of 'developing' debtor societies, because mandated cuts in public spending translate into fewer social programmes, reduced educational opportunities, more environmental pollution, and greater poverty for the vast majority of people.

Typically, the largest share of the developing countries' national budget is spent on servicing their outstanding debts. According to World Bank and OECD data, in 2010 alone, developing countries paid out $184 billion in debt service while receiving only $134 billion in aid. That year, the public external debt of the global South had reached $1.6 trillion (see Figure F). This sounds like a lot of money, but it represents only 5 per cent of the estimated $29 trillion the United States government spent on the bailout of the banks in the wake of the GFC. Pressured for decades by anti-corporate globalist forces like the Committee for the Abolition of Third-World Debt, the IMF and the World Bank were only recently willing to consider a new policy of blanket debt forgiveness in special cases.

As this chapter has shown, economic perspectives on globalization can hardly be discussed apart from an analysis of political process and institutions. After all, the intensification of global economic interconnections does not simply fall from the sky; rather, it is set in motion by a series of political decisions. Hence, while acknowledging the importance of economics in our story of globalization, this chapter nonetheless ends with the suggestion that we ought to be sceptical of one-sided accounts that identify expanding economic activity as the primary aspect of globalization. Rather, the impact of politics on the forging of global interconnectivity demands that we flesh out in more detail the political dimension of globalization.

Globalization

Total external debt of emerging and developing economies in 1970	US$70.2 billion
Total external debt of emerging and developing economies in 1980	US$569 billion
Total external debt of emerging and developing economies in 2013	US$6.857 trillion
Total external debt of emerging and developing economies in 2013 as a percentage of the total GDP	23.55%
Total external debt of emerging and developing economies in 2013 as a percentage of export goods and services	72.25%
Cost of the war in Iraq and Afganistan to the USA (2001–2012)	US$1.349 trillion
Cost to convert one billion households to renewable wind energy	US$1.2 trillion
Amount of global South debt the G8 promised to write off	US$100 billion
Amount of debt actually written off	US$46 billion
Number of countries eligible for the international Heavily Indebted Poor	36

Countries initiative (HIPC) in 2015	
Total amount of multilateral debt owned by the 36 HIPCs that is NOT eligible for cancellation	US$93 billion
Percentage of Lebanon's GDP spent on debt servicing	19%
Percentage of Lebanon's GDP spent on public health	4%
Mozambique's gross debt in 2014	US$7.8 billion
Mozambique's predicted gross debt in 2020	US$15 billion
Google's net profit in 2015	US$13.7 billion

F. The global South: a fate worse than debt.

Sources: IMF: <http://www.imf.org/external/pubs/ft/weo/2012/01/weodata/index.aspx>; CostofWar.com, 2012: <http://costofwar.com/>; Simon Murphy, 'Third of Debts Owed by Poor Countries to UK is Interest on Original Loans', *The Guardian*, 2012: <http://www.guardian.co.uk/world/2012/jan/22/poor-countries-debt-uk-interest>; Jubilee Campaign UK, Getting into Debt, 2010, p. 8: <http://jubileedebt.org.uk/countries>; Statista: <https://www.statista.com/search/?q=net+income>; Committee for the Abolition of Third World Debt: <cadtom.org/Overview-of-debt-in-the-South>; IMF 2015 Factsheet, 'Debt Relief under the Heavily Indebted Poor Countries (HIPC) Initiative': <http://www.imf.rog/external/np/exr/facts/hipc.htm>; Daniel Munevar and Eric Toussaint, 'The Debt of Developing Countries' (October 11, 2013): <http://www.globalresearch.ca/the-debt-of-developing-countries-the-devastating-impacts-of-imf-world-bank-economic medicine/5354027>

Chapter 4
The political dimension of globalization

Political globalization refers to the intensification and expansion of political interrelations across the globe. These processes raise an important set of political issues pertaining to the principle of state sovereignty, the growing impact of intergovernmental organizations, and the future prospects for regional and global governance, global migration flows, and environmental policies affecting our planet. Obviously, these themes respond to the evolution of political arrangements beyond the framework of the nation-state, thus breaking new conceptual and institutional ground. After all, for the last two centuries, humans have organized their political differences along territorial lines that generated a sense of 'belonging' to a particular nation-state.

This artificial division of planetary social space into 'domestic' and 'foreign' spheres corresponds to people's collective identities based on the creation of a common 'us' and an unfamiliar 'them'. Thus, the modern nation-state system has rested on psychological foundations and cultural assumptions that convey a sense of existential security and historical continuity, while at the same time demanding from its citizens that they put their national loyalties to the ultimate test. Nurtured by demonizing images of 'outsiders', people's belief in the superiority of their own nation has supplied the mental energy required for large-scale warfare—just as the enormous productive capacities of the modern state have provided the material means necessary to fight the 'total wars' of the last century.

Contemporary manifestations of globalization have led to the greater permeation of these old territorial borders, in the process also softening hard conceptual boundaries and cultural lines of demarcation. Emphasizing these tendencies, commentators belonging to the camp of globalizers have suggested that the period since the late 1960s has been marked by a radical deterritorialization of politics, rule-making, and governance. Considering such pronouncements premature at best and erroneous at worst, sceptics have not only affirmed the continued relevance of the nation-state as the political container of modern social life but have also pointed to the emergence of regional blocs as evidence for new forms of territorialization. Some of these critics have gone so far as to suggest that globalization is actually accentuating people's sense of nationality. As each group of global studies scholars presents different assessments of the fate of the modern nation-state, they also quarrel over the relative importance of political and economic factors.

Out of these disagreements there have emerged three fundamental questions that probe the extent of political globalization. First, is it really true that the power of the nation-state has been curtailed by massive flows of capital, people, and technology across territorial boundaries? Second, are the primary causes of these flows to be found in politics or in economics? Third, are we witnessing the emergence of new global governance structures? Before we respond to these questions in more detail, let us briefly consider the main features of the modern nation-state system.

The modern nation-state system

The origins of the modern nation-state system can be traced back to 17th-century political developments in Europe. In 1648, the Peace of Westphalia concluded a lengthy period of religious wars among the main European powers following the Protestant Reformation. Based on the newly formulated principles of sovereignty and territoriality, the ensuing model of self-contained, impersonal states challenged the medieval mosaic of small polities in which political power tended to be local and personal in focus but still subordinated to a larger imperial authority. The centuries following the Peace of Westphalia saw the further centralization of political power, the expansion of state administration, the development of professional diplomacy, and the successful monopolization of the means of coercion in the hands of the state. Moreover, nation-states also provided the military means required for the expansion of commerce, which, in turn, contributed to the spread of this European form of political rule around the globe.

The modern nation-state system found its mature expression at the end of the First World War in US President Woodrow Wilson's famous 'Fourteen Points' based on the principle of national self-determination. But Wilson's assumption that all forms of national identity should be given their territorial expression in a sovereign 'nation-state' proved to be extremely difficult to enforce in practice. Moreover, by enshrining the nation-state as the ethical and legal pinnacle of his proposed interstate system, he unwittingly lent some legitimacy to those radical ethnonationalist forces that pushed the world's main powers into the Second World War. Wilson's other idea of a 'League of Nations' that would give international cooperation an institutional expression was eventually realized with the founding of the United Nations in 1945 (see Illustration 9). While deeply rooted in a political order based on the modern nation-state system, the UN and other fledgling intergovernmental organizations also served as catalysts for the gradual extension of political activities across national boundaries, thus simultaneously affirming and undermining the principle of national sovereignty.

As globalization tendencies grew stronger during the 1970s and 1980s, it became clear that the international society of separate

9. The Security Council of the United Nations in session.

states was rapidly turning into a global web of political interdependencies that challenged conventional forms of national sovereignty.

In 1990, at the outset of the First Gulf War, US President George H. W. Bush announced the birth of a 'new world order' whose leaders no longer respected the idea that cross-border wrongful acts were a matter concerning only those states affected. Did this mean that the modern nation-state system based on national sovereignty and autonomy was no longer viable?

The demise of the nation-state?

Globalizers respond to this question affirmatively. At the same time, these observers consider political globalization a mere secondary phenomenon driven by more fundamental economic and technological forces. They argue that politics has been rendered almost powerless by an unstoppable techno-economic juggernaut that will crush all governmental attempts to reintroduce restrictive policies and regulations. Endowing economics with an inner logic apart from, and superior to, politics, these commentators look forward to a new phase in world history in which the main role of government will be to serve as a superconductor for global capitalism.

Pronouncing the rise of a 'borderless world', globalizers seek to convince the public that globalization inevitably involves the decline of bounded territory as a meaningful concept for understanding political and social change. Consequently, they suggest that political power is located in global social formations and expressed through global networks rather than through territorially based states. In fact, they argue that nation-states have already lost their dominant role in the global economy. As territorial divisions are becoming increasingly irrelevant, states are even less capable of determining the direction of social life within their borders. For example, since the workings of genuinely global capital markets dwarf their ability to control exchange rates or protect their currency, nation-states have become vulnerable to the discipline imposed by economic choices made elsewhere, over which states have no practical control.

The group of globalization sceptics disagrees, highlighting instead the central role of politics in unleashing the forces of globalization, especially through the successful mobilization of political power. In their view, the rapid expansion of global economic activity can be reduced neither to a natural law of the market nor to the development of computer technology. Rather, it originated with political decisions made by neoliberal national governments in the 1980s and 1990s to lift international restrictions on capital. Once those decisions were implemented, global markets and new technologies came into their own. The clear implication of this perspective is that national territory still matters. Hence, globalization sceptics insist on the continued relevance of conventional political units, operating in the form of either modern nation-states or global cities linked to national units.

The arguments of both globalizers and sceptics remain entangled in a particularly vexing version of the chicken-and-the-egg problem. After all, economic forms of interdependence are set in motion by political decisions, but these decisions are nonetheless made in particular economic contexts. As we noted, the economic and political aspects of globalization are profoundly interconnected. For example, it has become much easier for capital to escape taxation and other national policy restrictions. In 2016, the 'Panama Papers'—a leaked set of nearly 12 million confidential documents—revealed how wealthy individuals (including government officials) managed to evade national income taxes by hiding their assets in Panamanian offshore companies. Moreover, global markets frequently undermine the capacity of governments to set independent national policy objectives and impose their own domestic standards. Hence, it is difficult not to acknowledge the decline of the nation-state as a sovereign entity and the ensuing devolution of state power to regional and local governments as well as to various supranational institutions.

Political globalization and migration

On the other hand, the relative decline of the nation-state does not necessarily mean that governments have become impotent bystanders to the workings of global forces. States can still take measures to make their economies more or less attractive to global investors. In addition, they have continued to retain control over education, infrastructure, and foreign policy. But the intensifying population movements in the era of globalization have challenged some of the most crucial powers of nation-states: immigration control, population registration, and security protocols. Although in 2016 only 2 per cent of the world's population lived outside their country of origin, immigration control has become a central issue in most advanced nations. Many governments seek to restrict population flows, particularly those originating in the poor countries of the global South. Even in the United States, annual inflows of about 1 million legal permanent immigrants during the

2010s are less than the levels recorded during the first two decades of the 20th century.

In order to illustrate the growing problems of nation-states to cope with increasing trans-border migration flows, let us consider a recent example that has proven to be especially challenging: the Syrian refugee crisis. It started in March 2011 when, as part of the wider Arab Uprisings that swept across the Middle East region from Tunisia to the Gulf States, pro-democracy protests erupted in Syria that challenged the authoritarian rule of President Bashar al-Assad and his Baath Party. At first, Assad seemed to bow to mounting domestic foreign pressure to hold free elections and respect basic human rights. But once Russian President Vladimir Putin signalled his support, the Syrian dictator embarked on a confrontational course with pro-democracy demonstrators whom he vilified as 'rebel forces'. The country quickly descended into an all-out civil war that would kill more than 250,000 people over the next five years.

The relentless fighting triggered a humanitarian crisis of truly epic proportions. By 2016, nearly 6 million Syrians—out of a total population of 23 million—had been internally displaced. Close to 5 million people had fled the country in search of both personal safety and economic opportunity (see Map 4). The majority of Syrian refugees ended up in camps in the neighbouring countries of Jordan, Lebanon, Iraq, and Turkey, where they received some humanitarian assistance from local governments, international NGOs such as Mercy Corps and World Vision, and global institutions like the UN. Still, in most cases, the massive refugee flows pouring out of Syria strained the available material resources of host communities and also created significant cultural tensions with domestic populations who saw these 'outsiders' as a drain on their country's economic resources.

In recent years, hundreds of thousands of Syrian refugees have attempted the dangerous trip across the Mediterranean from

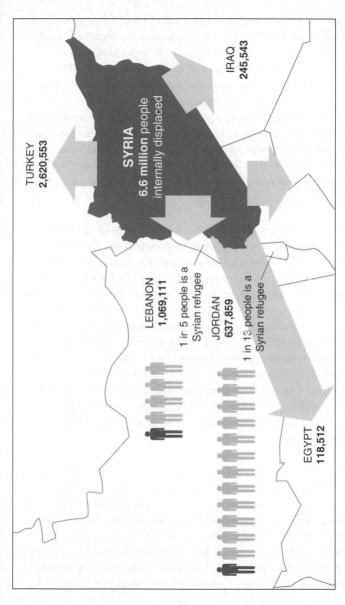

TURKEY
2,620,553

IRAQ
245,543

SYRIA
6.6 million people
internally displaced

LEBANON
1,069,111

1 ir 5 people is a
Syrian refugee

JORDAN
637,859

1 in 13 people is a
Syrian refugee

EGYPT
118,512

Map 4. The Syrian Refugee Crisis.

Turkey to Greece, hoping to find a better future in the prosperous states of the European Union. Germany, in particular, emerged as their preferred place of refuge. But in order to reach their destination, Syrian migrants had to embark on a long route that led them from Greece across Macedonia, Serbia or Croatia, Hungary or Slovenia, and Austria, until they finally arrived in Bavaria hoping for a swift approval of their residence applications. Even though some EU countries like Hungary resorted to rather inhumane policies and drastic measures to keep refugees out of their territory, their hastily erected border fences stretching over many miles ultimately proved to be ineffective in stopping such gigantic population movements.

In fact, the Syrian refugee crisis revealed the inadequacy of the EU's current institutional immigration arrangements based on national preferences. The so-called 'Schengen Agreement' that provided for open borders among EU core countries lacked the robustness and comprehensiveness necessary for coping with this crisis situation. As policy differences among various national governments became more pronounced, some member countries temporarily withdrew from the agreement and reinstituted systematic border controls. Others placed arbitrary limits on the number of refugees they were willing to process and refused to consider a more coordinated approach. Unable to deal with the huge influx of migrants, the EU faced a predicament that laid bare deep political divisions over migration policy among member states.

Moreover, the Syrian refugee crisis also made visible existing cultural fissures and biases. For example, a number of official government ministers in member states like Poland, Slovakia, and Hungary openly expressed their opposition to the 'Islamization of Europe' and stated their preference for Christian refugees. Countries like Germany and Austria, on the other hand, experienced a polarization of public sentiments with roughly even numbers of citizens supporting or opposing more liberal immigration measures. In the face of such politically explosive divisions, the conservative German government under Chancellor Angela Merkel showed tremendous courage and compassion by welcoming over 1 million refugees in 2015 alone—half of whom hailed from Syria. To put this remarkable number into perspective, this means that Germany accepted more Syrian refugees than the US refugee total for all political refugees for 2015. With additional social and political crises mounting in the global South, the migration crisis in Europe—and in many other parts of the world—is likely to continue for many years, even decades (see Illustration 10).

Finally, the intensifying global migration dynamics coupled with the activities of global terrorist networks—such as the 2015 Paris attacks or the 2016 Brussels bombings by local cells affiliated with ISIL—have revealed the inadequacy of conventional national security routines and protocols based on the modern nation-state system. The globalization of terrorist and crime networks has forced national governments to engage in new forms of

10. Syrian refugees protesting at a makeshift camp in Northern Greece, March 2016.

international cooperation. Thus, we can observe a seemingly paradoxical effect of political globalization: states still matter, but at the same time they are increasingly forced into transnational dynamics that undermine their old claims to national sovereignty and non-interference.

In summary, then, we ought to reject premature pronouncements of the impending demise of the nation-state, while also acknowledging its increasing difficulties in performing some of its traditional functions. Contemporary globalization has weakened some of the conventional boundaries between domestic and foreign policies while fostering the growth of supraterritorial social spaces and institutions that, in turn, unsettle both familiar political arrangements and cultural traditions. As the 21st century wears on, people around the world will become more conscious of the fact that they live in a transitional era moving from the modern nation-state system to postmodern forms of global governance.

Political globalization and global governance

Political globalization is perhaps most visible in the rise of supraterritorial institutions and associations held together by common norms and interests (see Figure G). In this early phase of global governance, these structures resemble an eclectic network of interrelated power centres such as municipal and provincial authorities, regional blocs, international organizations, and national and international private-sector associations.

On the municipal and provincial level, there has been a remarkable growth in the number of policy initiatives and trans-border links between various sub-state authorities. For example, Chinese provinces and US federal states have established permanent missions and points of contact, some of which operate relatively autonomously with little oversight from their respective national

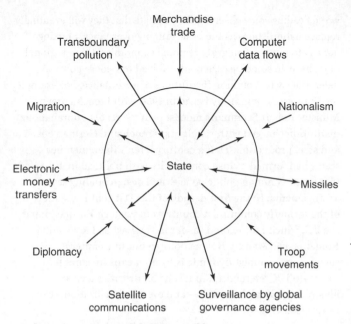

G. The nation-state in a globalizing world.

Source: Jan Aart Scholte, 'The globalization of world politics', in John Baylis and Steve Smith (eds), *The Globalization of World Politics*, 2nd edn (Oxford University Press, 2001), p. 22. With permission of Oxford University Press

governments. Various provinces and federal states in Canada, India, and Brazil are developing their own trade agendas and financial strategies to obtain loans. An example of international cooperation on the municipal level is the rise of powerful city networks like the World Association of Major Metropolises that develop cooperative ventures to deal with common local issues across national borders. 'Global cities' such as Hong Kong, London, New York, Shanghai, Singapore, Sydney, and Tokyo sometimes are more closely connected to each other than they are to their national governments.

On the regional level, there has been an extraordinary proliferation of multilateral organizations and agreements. Regional clubs and agencies such as APEC or ASEAN have sprung up across the world, leading some observers to speculate that they will eventually replace nation-states as the basic unit of governance. Starting out as attempts to integrate regional economies, these regional blocs have, in some cases, already evolved into loose political federations with common institutions of governance. For example, the European Community began in 1950 with French Foreign Minister Robert Schuman's modest plan to create a supranational institution charged with regulating French and German coal and steel production. Half a century later, fifteen member states had formed a close community with political institutions that create common public policies and design binding security arrangements. In the first decade of the 21st century, some of the formerly communist countries in Eastern Europe joined the EU, which now extends as far to the East as Latvia and Romania (see Map 5). But, as pointed out in Chapter 8, such an expansionist dynamic is by no means inexorable. The 2016 UK referendum in favour of 'Brexit' is a clear illustration that globalization—and even regionalization—can be reversed.

On a global level, governments have formed a number of international organizations, including the UN, NATO, WTO, and OECD. Full legal membership of these organizations is open to states only, and the decision-making authority lies with representatives from national governments. The proliferation of these transnational bodies has shown that nation-states find it increasingly difficult to manage sprawling networks of social interdependence.

Finally, the emerging structure of global governance has been shaped by 'global civil society'—a social realm populated by thousands of voluntary, non-governmental associations of worldwide reach. International NGOs like Doctors Without Borders or Greenpeace represent millions of ordinary citizens who are prepared to challenge political and economic decisions made by nation-states and intergovernmental organizations.

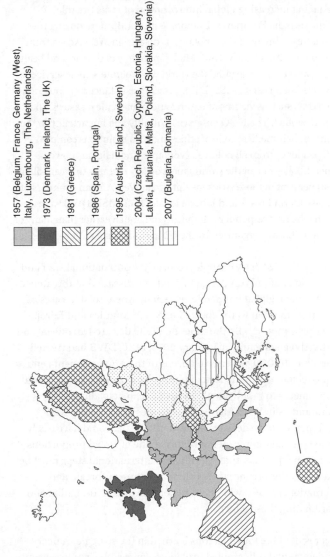

1957 (Belgium, France, Germany (West), Italy, Luxembourg, The Netherlands)

1973 (Denmark, Ireland, The UK)

1981 (Greece)

1986 (Spain, Portugal)

1995 (Austria, Finland, Sweden)

2004 (Czech Republic, Cyprus, Estonia, Hungary, Latvia, Lithuania, Malta, Poland, Slovakia, Slovenia)

2007 (Bulgaria, Romania)

Map 5. The European Union.

One concrete example of the growing significance of NGOs in managing increasing global interconnectivity was the role of Médicins Sans Frontières/Doctors Without Borders during the dramatic outbreak of the Ebola virus disease in West Africa from December 2013 to early 2016. Made up mainly of doctors and health sector workers from around the world who volunteer their services at any location on earth, MSF/DWB provides assistance to populations in distress such as victims of natural and man-made disasters, and armed conflict. The NGO observes neutrality and impartiality in the name of their medical code of ethics and also maintains complete independence from all political, economic, and religious powers. When Ebola—one of the world's most deadly diseases that can kill up to 90 per cent of those stricken—hit in the West African countries of Guinea, Sierra Leone, and Liberia in late 2013, MSF/DWB were among the first responders on the ground, much earlier than many of the aid initiatives organized by the UN or individual nation-states.

At its peak, MSF/DWF employed nearly 4,000 national staff and 325 expat staff in West Africa to combat a disease that threatened to turn into a global pandemic, especially when isolated cases of virus transmission were reported in North America and Europe (see Illustration 11). By the time the WHO declared an official end to the Ebola epidemic in January 2016, MSF/DWB had treated more than 10,000 patients in dozens of their management centres in the region. Given the lack of political will by national and local governments to rapidly deploy assistance to help affected communities in West Africa, the activities of NGOs like MSF/DWB proved to be decisive in preventing what could have easily turned into an unprecedented catastrophe of global proportions. There is no question that coordinated international steps must be taken to better prepare the world for a future outbreak, and international NGOs will play a major role in both designing and coordinating those efforts.

As a result of the tough lessons learned in the struggle against pandemics and other global problems, some global studies experts

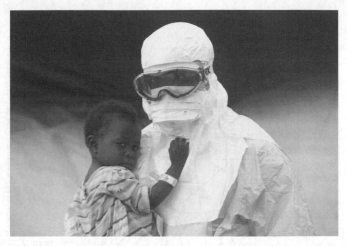

11. MSF health worker in Liberia holding a child suspected of having Ebola, October 2014.

believe that political globalization might facilitate the strengthening of democratic transnational social forces anchored in this thriving sphere of global civil society. Predicting that democratic rights will ultimately become detached from their narrow relationship to discrete territorial units, these optimistic voices anticipate the creation of a democratic global governance structure based on Western cosmopolitan ideals, international legal arrangements, and a web of expanding linkages between various governmental and non-governmental organizations. If such a promising scenario indeed comes to pass, then the final outcome of political globalization might well be the emergence of a 'cosmopolitan democracy' that would constitute the basis for a plurality of identities flourishing within a structure of mutual toleration and accountability (see Figure H).

According to David Held, one of the chief academic proponents of this view, such a cosmopolitan democracy of the future would contain the following features:

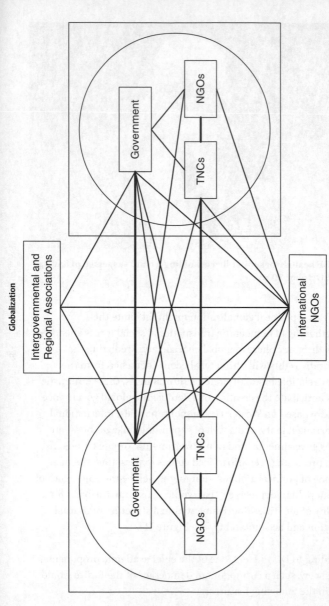

H. Incipient global governance: a network of interrelated power centres.

Source: adapted from Peter Willets, 'Transnational actors and international organizations in global politics', in Baylis and Smith, *The Globalization of World Politics*, 5th edn (Oxford University Press, 2011), p. 339. With permission of Oxford University Press

1. A global parliament connected to regions, states, and localities;
2. A new charter of rights and duties locked into different domains of political, social, and economic power;
3. The formal separation of political and economic interests;
4. An interconnected global legal system with mechanisms of enforcement from the local to the global.

A number of less optimistic commentators have challenged Held's idea that political globalization is moving in the direction of cosmopolitan democracy. Most criticisms boil down to the charge that his benign vision indulges in an abstract idealism that fails to engage current political tensions on the national level of public policy such as the clashing immigration perspectives within the EU. Global governance sceptics have also expressed the suspicion that the proponents of cosmopolitan democracy do not consider in sufficient detail its cultural feasibility. In other words, the worldwide intensification of cultural, political, and economic interactions makes the possibility of resistance and opposition just as real as the benign vision of mutual accommodation and tolerance of differences. To follow up on this cultural dimension of globalization, let us turn to Chapter 5.

Chapter 5
The cultural dimension of globalization

As our opening discussion of the 2014 FIFA World Cup has shown, even a *very short* introduction to globalization would be woefully inadequate without an examination of its cultural dimension. Cultural globalization refers to the intensification and expansion of cultural flows across the globe. Obviously, 'culture' is a very broad concept; it is frequently used to describe the whole of human experience. In order to avoid the ensuing problem of overgeneralization, it is important to make analytical distinctions between various aspects of social life. For example, we associate the adjective 'economic' with the production, exchange, and consumption of commodities. If we are discussing the 'political', we mean practices related to the generation and distribution of power in societies. If we are talking about the 'cultural', we are concerned with the symbolic construction, articulation, and dissemination of meaning. Given that language, music, and images constitute the major forms of symbolic expression, they assume special significance in the sphere of culture.

The exploding network of cultural interconnections and interdependencies in the last decades has led some commentators to suggest that cultural practices lie at the very heart of contemporary globalization. Yet, cultural globalization did not start with the worldwide dissemination of rock 'n' roll, Coca-Cola, or football. As noted in Chapter 2, expansive civilizational exchanges are much older than modernity. Still, the volume and extent of cultural transmissions in the 21st century have far exceeded those of earlier times. Facilitated by the Internet and our proliferating mobile digital devices, the dominant symbolic systems of meaning of our age—such as individualism, consumerism, and various religious discourses—circulate more freely and widely than ever before. As images and ideas can be more easily and rapidly transmitted from one place to another, they profoundly impact the way people experience their everyday lives. Today, cultural practices have escaped the prison of fixed localities such as town and nation, eventually acquiring new meanings in interaction with dominant global themes.

The thematic landscape traversed by scholars of cultural globalization is vast and the questions they raise are too numerous to be fleshed out in this short introduction. Rather than offering a long laundry list of relevant topics, this chapter will focus on three important themes: the tension between sameness and difference in the emerging global culture; the crucial role of transnational media corporations in disseminating popular culture; and the globalization of languages.

Global culture: sameness or difference?

Does globalization make people around the world more alike or more different? This is the question most frequently raised in discussions on the subject of cultural globalization. A group of commentators we might call 'pessimistic' globalizers argue in favour of the former. They suggest that we are not moving towards a cultural rainbow that reflects the diversity of the world's existing populations. Rather, we are witnessing the rise of an increasingly homogenized popular culture underwritten by a Western 'culture industry' based in New York, Hollywood, London, Paris, and Milan. As evidence for their interpretation, these commentators point to Amazonian Indians wearing Nike sneakers; denizens of the Southern Sahara purchasing Yankees baseball caps; and

Palestinian youths proudly displaying their Golden State Warriors basketball singlets in downtown Ramallah. Referring to the diffusion of Anglo-American values and consumer goods as the 'Americanization of the world', the proponents of this cultural homogenization thesis argue that Western norms and lifestyles are overwhelming more vulnerable cultures. Although there have been serious attempts by some countries to resist these forces of cultural imperialism—for example, a ban on satellite dishes in Iran, and the French imposition of tariffs and quotas on imported films and television programmes—the spread of American popular culture seems to be unstoppable.

But these manifestations of sameness are also evident inside the dominant countries of the global North. American sociologist George Ritzer coined the term 'McDonaldization' to describe the wide-ranging sociocultural processes by which the principles of the fast-food restaurant are coming to dominate more and more sectors of American society as well as the rest of the world. On the surface, these principles appear to be rational in their attempts to offer efficient and predictable ways of serving people's needs. However, looking behind the façade of repetitive TV commercials that claim to 'love to see you smile', we can identify a number of serious problems. For one, the generally low nutritional value of fast-food meals—and particularly their high fat content—has been implicated in the rise of serious health problems such as heart disease, diabetes, cancer, and juvenile obesity. Moreover, the impersonal, routine operations of 'rational' fast-service establishments actually undermine expressions of forms of cultural diversity. In the long run, the McDonaldization of the world amounts to the imposition of uniform standards that eclipse human creativity and dehumanize social relations (see Figure I).

One particular thoughtful analyst in this group of pessimistic globalizers is American political theorist Benjamin Barber. In his popular book *Consumed* (2007), he warns his readers against an 'ethos of infantilization' that sustains global capitalism, turning adults into children through dumbed-down advertising and consumer goods while also targeting children as consumers. This ethos is premised on the recognition that there is not an endless market for consumerist goods as was once thought. Global inequality contributes to stifling the growth of markets and of capitalism. In order to expand markets and make a profit, global capitalists are developing homogeneous global products targeting the young and wealthy throughout the world, as well as turning children into consumers. Thus, global consumerism becomes increasingly soulless and unethical in its pursuit of profit.

Optimistic globalizers agree with their pessimistic colleagues that cultural globalization generates more sameness, but they consider this outcome to be a good thing. For example, American social theorist Francis Fukuyama explicitly welcomes the global spread of Anglo-American values and lifestyles, equating the Americanization of the world with the expansion of democracy and free markets (see Illustration 12). But optimistic globalizers do not just come in the form of American nationalists who apply the old theme of manifest destiny to the global arena. Some representatives of this camp consider themselves staunch cosmopolitans who celebrate the Internet and the latest digital devices as the harbinger of a homogenized 'techno-culture'. Others are free-market enthusiasts who embrace the values of global consumer capitalism.

It is one thing to acknowledge the existence of powerful homogenizing tendencies in the world, but it is quite another to assert that the cultural diversity existing on our planet is destined to vanish. In fact, several influential commentators offer a contrary assessment that links globalization to new forms of cultural expression. Sociologist Roland Robertson, for example, contends that global cultural flows often reinvigorate local cultural niches.

Globalization

Average time Americans spend watching TV per day (2017)	282 minutes
Average time Americans spend socializing and face-to-face communicating per day (2014)	46 minutes
Advertising content shown per one hour of prime time TV (2013)	14 minutes and 15 seconds
Number of advertisements, logos and labels seen by the average American every day	16,000
Money spent by TV advertisers on commercials per year (2013)	$78 billion
Percentage of adult Americans who are obese (2012)	34.9%
The percentage of the average American's daily 'vegetable' intake that is made up of French fries	25%
Average annual intake of meat in the USA (vs India)	100 kg (5 kg)
Average number of cows in a single fast-food hamburger patty	55–1,082
Average number of hamburgers eaten in the US per week (2012)	3
Carbon dioxide produced to make one hamburger	3.6–6.1 kg CO_2
Carbon dioxide produced by the American hamburger consumption annually (more than Hungary's national CO_2 output)	65,250,000 metric tons CO_2

The number of other countries that contribute ingredients to the average American meal	5
The number of cars registered in the USA (2013)	256 million
Amount of rubbish produced by Americans (2013)	254 million tonnes
Total mass of living humans on Earth (2012)	287 million tonnes
Percentage of Americans who believe that God created humans in their present form less than 10,000 years ago (2012)	46%

I. The American way of life.

Sources: Leopold Center for Sustainable Agriculture, 2003, 'Checking the food odometer: Comparing food miles for local versus conventional produce sales to Iowa institutions':

<http://www.leopold.iastate.edu/sites/default/files/pubs-and-papers/20C3-07-checking-food-odometer- comparing-food-miles-local-versus-conventional-produce-sales-iowa-institution.pdf>; Centre for Disease Control and Prevention: <http://www.cdc.gov/obesity/data/adult.html>; Jamais Cascio, *The Cheeseburger Footprint*, 2012: <http://www.openthefuture.com/cheeseburger_CF.html>; Statista: <http://www.statista.com/statistics/271380/average-tv-viewing-time-in-north-america/>; Bureau of Labor Statistics, 2012: <http://www.bls.gov/news.release/atus.nr0.htm>; Dharma Singh Khalsa, *Brain Longevity*, Grand Central Publishing, p. 29; Norman Herr, *The Sourcebook for Teaching Science*, 2012: <http://www.csun.edu/science/health/docs/tv&health.html>; Statista: <http://www.statista.com/statistics/183505/number-of-vehicles-in-the-united-states-since-1990/>; Statista: <http://www.statista.com/statistics/189527/daily-time-spent-on-socialiing-and-communicating-in-the-us- since-2009/>; Gallup Poll, Evolution, Creationism, Intelligent Design, 2012: <http://www.gallup.com/poll/21814/evolution-creationism-intelligent-design.aspx>; TV Week: <http://www.tweek.com/tvbizwire/2014/05/how-many-minutes-of-commercial/>; Environmental Protection Agency: <https://www.epa.gov/smm/advancing-sustainable-materials-management-facts-and-figures>; Michael Marshal, 'Humanity weighs in at 287 million tonnes', 2012: <http://www.newscientist.com/article/dn21945-humanity-weighs-in-at-287-million-tonnes.html>

12. **Jihad vs McWorld: selling fast food in Indonesia.**

Hence, rather than being totally obliterated by the Western consumerist forces of sameness, local difference and particularity still play an important role in creating unique cultural constellations. Arguing that cultural globalization always takes place in local contexts, Robertson rejects the cultural homogenization thesis and speaks instead of glocalization—the complex globalization dynamic involving the interaction of the global and local. The resulting expressions of cultural 'hybridity' cannot be reduced to clear-cut manifestations of 'sameness' or 'difference'. As we noted in our discussion of Lionel Messi and J. Lo in Chapter 1, such processes of hybridization have become most visible in fashion, music, dance, film, food, sports, and language.

But the respective arguments of globalizers and sceptics are not necessarily incompatible. The contemporary experience of living and acting across cultural borders means both the loss of traditional meanings and the creation of new symbolic expressions. Reconstructed feelings of belonging coexist in uneasy tension with a sense of placelessness. Indeed, some commentators have argued that modernity is slowly giving way to a new 'postmodern' framework characterized by a less stable sense of identity, place, and knowledge.

Given the complexity of global cultural flows, one would actually expect to see uneven and contradictory effects. In certain contexts, these flows might change traditional manifestations of national identity in the direction of a popular culture characterized by sameness; in others they might foster new expressions of cultural particularism; in still others they might encourage forms of cultural hybridity. Those commentators who summarily denounce the homogenizing effects of Americanization must not forget that hardly any society in the world today possesses an 'authentic', self-contained culture. Those who despair at the flourishing of cultural hybridity ought to listen to exciting Bollywood pop songs, admire the intricacy of several variations of Hawaiian pidgin, or enjoy the culinary delights of Cuban-Chinese cuisine. Finally, those who applaud the spread of consumerist capitalism need to pay attention to its negative consequences, such as the dramatic decline of traditional communal sentiments as well as the commodification of society and nature.

The role of the media

To a large extent, the global cultural flows of our time are generated and directed by global media empires that rely on powerful communication technologies to spread their message. Saturating global cultural reality with formulaic TV shows and mindless advertisements, these corporations increasingly shape people's identities and the structure of desires around the world. The rise of the global imaginary is inextricably connected to the rise of the global media. During the last two decades, a small group of very large TNCs have come to dominate the global market for entertainment, news, television, and film. In 2014, the eight largest media conglomerates—Comcast, Google, Disney, News Corporation, DirecTV, Viacom, Time Warner, and SONY—accounted for more than two-thirds of the $1.5 trillion in annual worldwide revenues generated by the global telecommunications industry.

As recently as fifteen years ago, many of the giant corporations that dominate what Benjamin Barber has appropriately called the 'infotainment telesector' did not exist in their present form as a media company. Today, most media analysts concede that the emergence of a global commercial-media market amounts to the creation of a global oligopoly similar to that of the oil and automotive industries in the early part of the 20th century. The crucial cultural innovators of earlier decades—small, independent record labels, radio stations, movie theatres, newspapers, and book publishers—have become virtually extinct as they found themselves incapable of competing with the media giants.

The commercial values disseminated by transnational media enterprises not only secure the undisputed cultural hegemony of popular culture, but also lead to the depoliticization of social reality and the weakening of civic bonds. One of the most glaring developments of the last two decades has been the transformation of news broadcasts and educational programmes into shallow entertainment shows—many of them ironically touted as 'reality shows'. Given that news is less than half as profitable as entertainment, media firms are increasingly tempted to pursue higher profits by ignoring journalism's much vaunted separation of newsroom practices and business decisions. Partnerships and alliances between news and entertainment companies are fast becoming the norm, making it more common for publishing executives to press journalists to cooperate with their newspapers' business operations. A sustained attack on the professional autonomy of journalism is, therefore, also part of cultural globalization.

The globalization of languages

One direct method of measuring and evaluating cultural changes brought about by globalization is to study the shifting global patterns of language use. The globalization of languages can be viewed as a process by which some languages are increasingly used in international communication while others lose their prominence and even disappear for lack of speakers. Researchers at the Globalization Research Center at the University of Hawai'i have identified five key variables that influence the globalization of languages:

1. *Number of languages*: The declining number of languages in different parts of the world points to the strengthening of homogenizing cultural forces.

2. *Movements of people*: People carry their languages with them when they migrate and travel. Migration patterns affect the spread of languages.

3. *Foreign language learning and tourism*: Foreign language learning and tourism facilitate the spread of languages beyond national or cultural boundaries.

4. *Internet languages*: The Internet has become a global medium for instant communication and quick access to information. Language use on the Internet is a key factor in the analysis of the dominance and variety of languages in international communication.

5. *International scientific publications*: International scientific publications contain the languages of global intellectual discourse, thus critically impacting intellectual communities involved in the production, reproduction, and circulation of knowledge around the world.

Given these highly complex interactions, research in this area frequently yields contradictory conclusions. Unable to reach a general agreement, experts in the field have developed several different hypotheses. One model posits a clear correlation between the growing global significance of a few languages—particularly English, Chinese, and Spanish—and the declining number of other languages around the world. Another model suggests that

Continents	Early 16th Century	Early 17th Century	Early 18th Century	Early 19th Century	Early 20th Century	Late 20th Century
Americas	2,175	2,025	1,800	1,500	1,125	1,005
Africa	4,350	4,050	3,600	3,000	2,250	2,011
Europe	435	405	360	300	225	201
Asia	4,785	4,455	3,960	3,300	2,475	2,212
Pacific	2,755	2,565	2,280	1,900	1,425	1,274
World	14,500	13,500	12,000	10,000	7,500	6,703

J. The declining number of languages around the world, 1500–2000.

Source: Globalization Research Center at the University of Hawai'i-Mānoa.

the globalization of language does not necessarily mean that our descendants are destined to utilize only a few tongues. Still another thesis emphasizes the power of the Anglo-American culture industry to make English—or what some commentators call 'Globish'—*the* global lingua franca of the 21st century.

To be sure, the rising significance of the English language has a long history, reaching back to the birth of British colonialism in the late 16th century. At that time, only approximately seven million people used English as their mother tongue. By the 1990s, this number had swollen to over 350 million native speakers, with 400 million more using English as a second language. Today, more than 80 per cent of the content posted on the Internet is in English. Almost half of the world's growing population of foreign students is enrolled at institutions in Anglo-American countries.

At the same time, however, the number of spoken languages in the world has dropped from about 14,500 in 1500 to about 6,400 in 2016 (see Figure J). Given the current rate of decline, some linguists predict that 50–90 per cent of the currently existing languages will have disappeared by the end of the 21st century. But the world's languages are not the only entities threatened with extinction. The spread of consumerist values and materialist lifestyles has endangered the ecological health of our planet as well.

Chapter 6
The ecological dimension of globalization

Although we have examined the economic, political, and cultural aspects of globalization separately, it is important to remember that each of these dimensions impacts on and has consequences for the other domains. Nowhere is this more clearly demonstrated than in the ecological dimensions of globalization. In recent years, global environmental issues such as global climate change and transboundary pollution have received enormous attention from research institutes, the media, politicians, economists, and the public in general. The ecological effects of globalization are now recognized as potentially life threatening for life on our planet. The worldwide impact of natural and man-made disasters such as the horrifying nuclear plant accidents at Chernobyl, Ukraine (1986) and Fukushima, Japan (2011) clearly shows that the formidable ecological problems of our time can only be tackled by a global alliance of states and civil society actors.

In the 21st century, it has become virtually impossible to ignore the fact that people everywhere on our planet are inextricably linked to each other through the air they breathe, the climate they depend upon, the food they eat, and the water they drink. In spite of this obvious lesson of interdependence, our planet's ecosystems are subjected to continuous human assault in order to maintain wasteful lifestyles. Indeed, cultural values greatly influence how people view their natural environment. For example, cultures steeped in Taoist, Buddhist, and various animist religions tend to emphasize the interdependence of all living beings—a perspective that calls for a delicate balance between human wants and ecological needs. Judaeo-Christian humanism, on the other hand, contains deeply dualistic values that put humans in control of nature. In Western modernity, the environment has thus come to be considered as a 'resource' to be used instrumentally to fulfil human needs and wants. The most extreme manifestation of this 'anthropocentric' paradigm is reflected in the dominant values and beliefs of consumerism. The capitalist culture industry seeks to convince its global audience that the meaning and chief value of life can be found in the limitless accumulation of material goods. Granted, some of the major ecological challenges the world faces today are problems that afflicted civilizations even in ancient times. But until the coming of the Industrial Revolution, environmental degradation was relatively localized and occurred slowly over many centuries.

In the last few decades, however, the scale, speed, and depth of Earth's environmental decline have been unprecedented. Let us briefly consider some of the most dangerous manifestations of the globalization of environmental degradation.

Two major concerns relate to uncontrolled population growth and lavish consumption patterns in the global North. Since farming economies first came into existence about 480 generations ago, the global population has exploded a thousand-fold to reach nearly 7.5 billion in 2017. Half of this increase has occurred in the last thirty years. With the possible exception of some rodent species, humans are now the most numerous mammals on earth. Vastly increased demands for food, timber, and fibre have put severe pressure on the planet's ecosystems.

Large areas of the Earth's surface, especially in arid and semi-arid regions, have been used for agricultural production for millennia, yielding crops for ever-increasing numbers of people. Concerns about the relationship between population growth and environmental degradation are frequently focused rather narrowly on aggregate population levels. Yet, the global impact of humans on the environment is as much a function of per capita consumption as it is of overall population size (see Figure K). For example, the United States comprises only 6 per cent of the world's population, yet it consumes 30–40 per cent of our planet's natural resources. Together, regional overconsumption and uncontrolled population growth present a serious problem to the health of our planet. Unless we are willing to change the underlying cultural and religious value structure that sustains these ominous dynamics, the health of Mother Earth is likely to deteriorate further.

	Annual oil consumption per capita (in litres)	Automobiles per 1,000 people	Annual meat consumption per capita (in kg)	Annual withdrawal of fresh water per capita (in cubic metres)
USA	3,504	808	123	1,518
South Korea	2,606	379	54	525
Finland	2,397	591	73	436
Brazil	572	259	80	297
Egypt	513	43	22	809
Indonesia	302	79	11	356
DR Congo	10	5	5	5

K. Annual consumption patterns (per capita) in selected countries (2012).

Sources: Oil: *CIA World Factbook*, 2012: <https://www.cia.gov/library/publications/the-world-factbook/index.html>; Cars: World Bank, 2012: <http://data.worldbank.org/indicator/IS.VEH.NVEH.P3>; Meat: UN Food and Agriculture Organization, 2010, *Livestock and Fish Primary Equivalent*:
<http://faostat.fao.org/site/291/default.aspx>; Water: Pacific Institute, *Worldwater.org*:
<http://www.worldwater.org/images/pdf.gif>

Some of the effects of overconsumption and population growth are painfully obvious in the current food crisis plaguing vast regions of our planet. Large-scale food riots in Haiti, Indonesia, the Philippines, China, and Cameroon in the last few years highlight increasing limitations on access to food in part as a result of environmental problems such as drought. Other factors include rising oil prices (which affect the cost of transportation of food), diversion of food staples such as corn into production of biofuels in efforts to reduce reliance on petroleum, and unequal access to resources across developed and developing countries. The current food crisis highlights the interconnections between political, economic, and ecological problems that are accentuated by the process of globalization.

Another significant ecological problem associated with population increases and the globalization of environmental degradation is the worldwide reduction of biodiversity. Seven out of ten biologists today believe that the world is now in the midst of the fastest mass extinction of living species in the 4.5-billion-year history of the planet. According to recent Organization for Economic Cooperation and Development (OECD) reports, two-thirds of the world's farmlands have been rated as 'somewhat degraded' and one-third have been marked as 'strongly degraded'. Half the world's wetlands have already been destroyed, and the biodiversity of freshwater ecosystems is under serious threat. Three-quarters of worldwide genetic diversity in agricultural crop and animal breeds has been lost since 1900. Some experts fear that up to 50 per cent of all plant and animal species—most of them in the global South—will disappear by the end of this century. Hence, many environmentalists have argued that biodiversity should be treated as a planetary asset and held in trust for the benefit of future generations.

Some of the measures currently undertaken to safeguard biodiversity include the creation of hundreds of 'gene banks' located in over a hundred countries around the world. One of the most spectacular of these banks is the Svalbard Global Seed Vault buried in permafrost in a mountain on the Arctic island of Spitzbergen. Officially opened in 2008, this 'Doomsday Vault' was funded by The Global Crop Diversity Trust (financed by international donors like the Gates and Rockefeller Foundations) and specially designed to store back-up copies of the seeds of the world's major food crops at minus 18 degrees Celsius. Operating like a safety deposit box in a bank, the Global Seed Vault is free of charge to public and private depositors and kept safe by the Norwegian government. But it is doubtful that such laudable 'back-up' measures are sufficient to reverse the escalating loss of biodiversity brought about by humanity's ecological footprint.

Transboundary pollution represents another grave danger to our collective survival. The release of vast amounts of synthetic chemicals into the air and water has created conditions for human and animal life that are outside previous limits of biological experience. For example, chlorofluorocarbons were used in the second half of the 20th century as non-flammable refrigerants, industrial solvents, foaming agents, and aerosol propellants. In the mid-1970s, researchers noted that the unregulated release of CFCs into the air seemed to be depleting Earth's protective ozone layer. A decade later, the discovery of large 'ozone holes' over Tasmania, New Zealand, and large parts of the Antarctic finally resulted in a coordinated international effort to phase out production of CFCs and other ozone-depleting substances. Scientists have warned that the risk of damage to the world's ozone layer has increased as a result of more frequent and severe storms and other 'extreme weather events' associated with global climate change. Other forms of transboundary pollution include industrial emissions of sulphur and nitrogen oxides. Returning to the ground in the form of acid rain, these chemicals damage forests, soils, and freshwater ecosystems. Current acid deposits in Northern Europe and parts of North America are at least twice as high as the critical level suggested by environmental agencies.

Finally, the issue of human-induced climate change has emerged as *the* major focus of domestic and intergovernmental policy as well as grass roots activism. Brought to public attention by former US Vice President Al Gore in the 2000s through his award-winning documentary *An Inconvenient Truth*—as well as the production of numerous scientific reports outlining the dire consequences of unchecked global warming—climate change is clearly one of the top global problems facing humanity today.

But perhaps the most influential recent attempt to raise people's consciousness about the dangers of climate change came from an unexpected quarter: the Vatican in Rome. In September 2015, Pope Francis I stood before the UN General Assembly and issued a radical call for the world to address global warming (see Illustration 13). Connecting the issue of climate change to the wider pursuit of equality, security, and social justice, the pontiff went so far as to send his shoes to the 2015 UNIPCC Climate Summit in Paris, to be displayed at the city's Place de la République together with thousands of shoes of other climate-change protesters as a public symbol to curb carbon emissions (see Box 7).

13. Pope Francis I addresses the UN General Assembly on climate change, 25 September 2015.

Box 7 Pope Francis's Climate Appeal

'I urgently appeal, then, for a new dialogue about how we are shaping the future of our planet. We need a conversation which includes everyone, since the environmental challenge we are undergoing, and its human roots, concern and affect us all. The worldwide ecological movement has already made considerable progress and led to the establishment of numerous organizations committed to raising awareness of these challenges. Regrettably, many efforts to seek concrete solutions to the environmental crisis have proved ineffective, not only because of powerful opposition but also because of a more general lack of interest. Obstructionist attitudes, even on the part of believers, can range from denial of the problem to indifference, nonchalant resignation or blind confidence in technical solutions. We require a new and universal solidarity.'

Excerpt from *Laudato Si* ('Praise Be to You'), Encyclical Letter issued by Pope Francis I on 24 May 2015.

The consequences of worldwide climate change, especially global warming, could be catastrophic. A large number of scientists worldwide are calling for concerted action by governments to curb greenhouse gas emissions. Indeed, global warming represents a grim example of the decisive shift in both the intensity and extent of contemporary environmental problems. The rapid build-up of gas emissions, including carbon dioxide, methane, nitrous and sulphur oxides, and chlorofluorocarbons, in our planet's atmosphere has greatly enhanced Earth's capacity to trap heat. The resulting 'greenhouse effect' is responsible for raising average temperatures worldwide (see Illustration 14).

The precise effects of global warming are difficult to calculate. Drawing on data collected by NOAA and the UNIPCC, a 2016 National Defense Council report predicts that global average

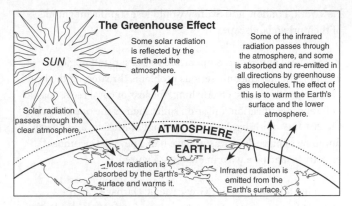

The Greenhouse Effect

Some solar radiation is reflected by the Earth and the atmosphere.

Some of the infrared radiation passes through the atmosphere, and some is absorbed and re-emitted in all directions by greenhouse gas molecules. The effect of this is to warm the Earth's surface and the lower atmosphere.

SUN

Solar radiation passes through the clear atmosphere.

ATMOSPHERE

EARTH

Most radiation is absorbed by the Earth's surface and warms it.

Infrared radiation is emitted from the Earth's surface.

14. The greenhouse effect.

temperatures in 2100 will be up to 8 degrees Fahrenheit warmer than today—should global emissions continue on their current path. Evidence shows that the decade from 2000 to 2010 was hotter than any other decade in the last 1,300 years. The 'Stern Report', commissioned by the UK government, asserted already in 2007 that average global temperatures had risen by at least 0.5 degrees Celsius based on pre-industrialization temperatures. Higher temperatures are worsening many kinds of extreme weather events, including storms, wild fires, floods, and droughts. And such disasters caused by global climate change not only endanger human lives but cause trillions of dollars of damage.

These significant increases in global temperatures have also led to meltdowns of large chunks of the world's major ice reserves. The polar ice caps have melted faster in the last twenty years than in the last 10,000. The large Greenland ice sheet is shrinking the fastest, and its complete melting would result in a global rise of sea levels of up to 22 feet. However, even a much smaller sea level rise would spell doom for many coastal regions around the world. The small Pacific island nations of Tuvalu and Kiribati, for example, would disappear. Large coastal cities such as Tokyo,

New York, London, and Sydney would lose significant chunks
of their urban landscapes.

But sea level and water temperature rise as a result of global
warming are not the only serious problems threatening the health
of our planet's oceans. Overfishing, the loss of coral reefs, coastal
pollution, acidification, mega-oil spills such as the one following
the 2010 BP oil rig explosion in the Gulf of Mexico, and illegal
dumping of hazardous wastes have had a devastating impact
on Earth's marine environments (see Figure L).

Consider, for example, the 'Great Pacific Garbage Patch'—a
gigantic floating mass of often toxic, non-biodegradable plastics
and chemical sludge twice the size of Texas that circulates
permanently in the powerful currents of the Northern Pacific

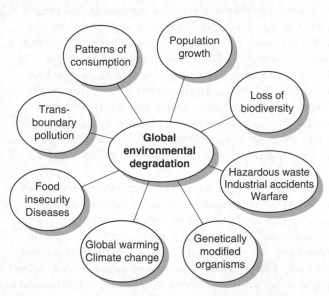

**L. Major manifestations and consequences of global environmental
degradation.**

Ocean. Or, perhaps even more horrifying, take the huge floating debris field generated by the devastating Japanese earthquake and tsunami of March 2011 that killed more than 15,000 people across Japan. The disaster caused the partial destruction of the Fukushima Daiichi nuclear plant, in the process allowing the escape of harmful radioactive particles into air and water. Stretching for nearly 2,000 miles and still containing 1.5 million tons of detritus (3.5 million tons have already sunk), this debris field crossed the Pacific in only fifteen months.

It deposited on North America's Pacific coast massive amounts of partially toxic materials such as wall insulation, oil and gas canisters, car tyres, fishing nets, and Styrofoam buoys. Heavier items are drifting underwater and might wash up in years to come. Experts fear that some of these materials might exceed safe levels of radioactivity. The debris field circled back to Hawai'i and Japan, between 2013 and 2016, only to start anew its ominous journey toward the Pacific shores of North America in 2017.

The central feature of all these potentially disastrous environmental problems is that they are 'global', thus making them serious problems for all sentient beings inhabiting our magnificent blue planet. Indeed, transboundary pollution, global warming, climate change, and species extinction are challenges that cannot be contained within national or even regional borders. They do not have isolated causes and effects, for they are caused by aggregate collective human actions and thus require a coordinated global response.

To be sure, ecological problems aggravated by globalization also have significant economic ramifications. Although these effects will be more significant for less developed countries than for rich countries, they will nonetheless affect all people and all nations. Poor countries do not have the necessary infrastructure or income to adapt to the unavoidable climate changes that will occur because of carbon emissions already in the earth's atmosphere. As we noted, developing regions are already warmer on average than most developed countries and consequently suffer from a high degree of variability in rainfall. To make matters worse, less developed countries are also heavily dependent on agriculture for the majority of their income. Since agriculture is the most climate sensitive of all economic sectors, developing nations will be more adversely affected by climate change than developed countries.

Further consequences of this vicious circle include increased illnesses, escalating death rates, and crumbling infrastructure. The cost of living will continue to rise, leaving poor households and communities unable to save for future emergencies. Recent scientific reviews like the Stern Report explicitly link the problem of climate change to development and aid provision in poor countries. They will require assistance from the developed world if they are to adapt and survive climate change. Thus, climate change and global warming are not merely environmental or scientific issues. They are economic, political, cultural, but, above all, ethical issues that have been expanded and intensified by the process of globalization.

There has been much debate in public and academic circles about the severity of climate change and the best ways for the global community to respond to it. As can be gleaned from the list of major global environmental treaties, international discussion on the issue of global warming and environmental degradation has been occurring for over thirty years. Yet, while much has been written and spoken about this issue, few coordinated measures have been implemented. Most international environmental treaties still lack effective enforcement mechanisms.

For the most part, political efforts in favour of immediate change have been limited. However, the most significant obstacles to the creation and implementation of an effective global environmental agreement have come from the unwillingness of China and the

United States—the world's two largest polluters—to ratify key agreements. Both nations see measures to reduce carbon emissions and thereby slow global warming as threats to their economic growth. Yet inaction on climate change today will have more dire consequences for economic growth tomorrow (see Figures M and N).

Still, there are some grounds for guarded optimism. For example, significant agreement exists that certain limitations on carbon emissions must be placed on all nations. Some rich countries in the EU—and Australia—managed to impose a national carbon tax on emitters. But poor countries argue that they should not be bound by the same carbon measures or trading schemes as developed countries. They make this argument for two reasons. First, they need to build up their industries and infrastructures in

Country	Total emissions (kilo tons of CO_2)	Per capita emissions (tonnes per capita)
China (mainland)	10,540,000	7.6
United States of America	5,334,000	16.5
India	2,341,000	1.8
Russian Federation	1,766,000	12.4
Japan	1,278,000	10.1
Germany	767,000	9.3
Islamic Republic of Iran	618,000	7.9
Republic of Korea	610,000	12.3
Canada	565,000	15.9
Brazil	501,000	2.5
Global total	35,669,000	5.0

M. The top ten carbon dioxide emitters, 2014.

Sources: PBL Netherlands Environmental Assessment Agency (2015): Olivier, J. G. J., Janssens-Maenhout, G., Muntean, M. Peters, J. H. A. W., Trends in global CO2 emissions – 2015 report, JRC report 98184 / PBL report 1803, November 2015:
<http://edgar.jrc.ec.europa.eu/overview.php?v=CO2ts_pc1990-2014>; and
<http://edgar.jrc.ec.europa.eu/overview.php?v=CO2ts1990-2014>

Year	Million metric tonnes of carbon
1750	3
1800	8
1850	54
1900	534
1950	1,630
2000	23,650
2014	37,500

N. Long-term global CO_2 emissions.

Source: Olivier J. G. J. et al. (2015), Trends in global CO2 emissions; 2015 Report, The Hague: PBL Netherlands Environmental Assessment Agency; Ispra: European Commission, Joint Research Centre

order to pull themselves out of poverty. Placing significant carbon emissions restrictions on their industries would seriously impede their economic development. Secondly, they argue that poor countries have not been responsible for the production of most of the greenhouse gases that have caused the current problem. Identifying developed countries as the primary producers of greenhouse gases, they suggest that the major burden for limiting the production of greenhouse gases should fall on the developed world—at least until developing countries have pulled their populations out of extreme poverty.

The United States has expressed strong opposition to these arguments by insisting that all countries should be subjected to the same limitations on carbon emissions. At the Thirteenth Conference of the Parties (COP 13) to the United Nations Framework Convention on Climate Change (UNFCCC) in Bali 2007, the US delegation repeatedly blocked negotiations by demanding that developing countries take more responsibility for their contribution to global warming. At the same time, however, America has been reluctant to enter into any agreement that might slow its own economic growth. Throughout the 2000s, the Bush administration walked away from key international treaties such as the Kyoto Protocol while remaining significantly behind other developed countries in its commitments on capping and reducing carbon emissions.

Unfortunately, the next US government did not fundamentally break with the approach of its predecessor. Although President Barack Obama made stronger rhetorical gestures in favour of environmental protection, his actions did not match his words. For example, at the 2009 Copenhagen Climate Summit, Obama acquiesced to unspecific, non-legally binding agreements that fell far short of the Summit's goal to establish a strong and binding global climate agreement.

In the same vein, the much anticipated 2012 UN conference on Sustainable Development in Brazil—known as Rio + 20 because it was held twenty years after the historic 1992 Rio Summit on Climate Change—merely produced toothless documents that paid lip service to a 'common vision' of environmental sustainability but failed to mandate binding emission reduction targets. National states proved themselves to be unwilling to engage in the sort of environmental multilateralism that would produce measurable results in the worldwide struggle against global warming.

In December 2015, however, the UN Framework Convention on Climate Change summit held in Paris, France, proved to be a turning point for action to limit climate change with an expressed objective to move to a zero carbon world within the foreseeable future. Uniting all of the world's nations in a single agreement on tackling climate change for the first time in history, the Paris 'global climate deal' comprised a number of key elements. First, the parties committed themselves to arresting the rise of global temperatures. Second, they pledged to limit the amount of greenhouse gases emitted by human activity to the same levels that trees, soil, and oceans can absorb naturally, beginning at some point between 2050 and 2100. Third, countries agreed to review each other's contribution to cutting emissions every five years so as to scale up the challenge. Finally, rich countries promised to help poorer nations by providing 'climate finance' to adapt to climate change and switch to renewable energy. While the final signing of the Paris Agreement in 2016 constitutes an important milestone in the global struggle for environmental sustainability, it nonetheless represents only the first step on the long road to a zero carbon world powered by non-fossil energy sources such as solar, wind, and wave. In 2018, the parties will meet again to assess their progress, with further review meetings scheduled every five years.

In their comprehensive study *Globalization and the Environment* (2013), the Australian political scientists Peter Christoff and Robyn Eckersley have identified five deep-seated and interlocking problems that stand in the way of an effective global environmental treaty system:

1. States have failed to integrate environmental and economic governance at the national level.

2. States have failed to integrate environmental and economic governance at the international level.

3. Powerful social forces continue to resist or co-opt efforts to transform economies and societies in a more ecologically sustainable direction.

4. The neoliberal economic discourse remains globally dominant, undermining sustainable development and ecological modernization discourses and practices.

5. All of the above persists because national and international accountability mechanisms remain weak and inadequate in a globalizing world.

The 2015 Paris agreement only addresses some of these points. Moreover, not all of the provisions of the treaty are legally binding, which means that international peer pressure constitutes the most effective form of enforcement available for addressing domestic

Name of Treaty/Conference	Coverage/protection	Date
UNESCO-World Heritage, Paris	Cultural and natural heritage	1972
UNEP Conference, Stockholm	General environment	1972
CITES, Washington, D.C.	Endangered species	1973
Marine pollution treaty, London	Marine pollution from ships	1978
UN Convention on Law of the Sea	Marine species, pollution	1982
Vienna Protocol	Ozone layer	1985
Montreal Protocol	Ozone layer	1987
Basel Convention	Hazardous wastes	1989
UN 'Rio Summit' on Environmental Climate Change	Biodiversity	1992
Jakarta Mandate	Marine and coastal diversity	1995
Kyoto Protocol	Global warming	1997
Rotterdam Convention	Industrial pollution	1998
Johannesburg World Summit	Ecological sustainability, pollution	2002
Bali Action Plan	Global warming	2007
UN Copenhagen Climate Summit	Global warming	2009
UN Cancun Climate Summit	Global warming	2010
UN Durban Climate Summit	Global warming	2011
UN Rio + 20	Sustainable development	2012
UN Paris Climate Summit	Climate change	2015

O. **Major global environmental treaties/conferences, 1972–2015.**

activities that are protected by national sovereignty. Thus, the negotiations over climate change serve as an instructive example for how the various dimensions of globalization intersect. In this case political globalization simply has not kept up with the demands of ecological globalization.

But time is of the essence. Some leading scientists believe that a further decade or two of slow, gradual action would make it impossible to avoid the disastrous impacts of climate change and ecological degradation (see Figure O). Confronted with the ill health of our Mother Earth in the second decade of the 21st century, it has become abundantly clear to many people that the contemporary phase of globalization has been the most environmentally destructive period in human history. It remains to be seen, however, whether the growing recognition of the ecological limits of our planet will translate swiftly into profound new forms of political cooperation across borders. As we will discuss in Chapter 7, much depends on challenging a powerful global ideology that is rooted in the utopia of unfettered markets and the desire for the unlimited accumulation and consumption of material things.

Chapter 7
Ideologies of globalization: market globalism, justice globalism, religious globalisms

Ideologies are powerful systems of widely shared ideas and patterned beliefs that are accepted as truth by significant groups in society. Serving as political mental maps, they offer people a more or less coherent picture of the world not only as it is, but also as it ought to be. In doing so, ideologies help organize the tremendous complexity of human experiences into fairly simple claims that serve as guide and compass for social and political action. These claims are employed to legitimize certain political interests and to defend or challenge dominant power structures. Seeking to imbue society with their preferred norms and values, the codifiers of ideologies—usually social elites—speak to their audience in narratives that persuade, praise, condemn, distinguish 'truths' from 'falsehoods', and separate the 'good' from the 'bad'. Thus, ideology connects theory and practice by orienting and organizing human action in accordance with generalized claims and codes of conduct.

Like all social processes, globalization operates on an ideological dimension filled with a range of norms, claims, beliefs, and narratives about the phenomenon itself. Indeed, the heated public debate over whether globalization represents a 'good' or a 'bad' thing occurs in the arena of ideology. Today, three types of globalism compete for adherents around the world. *Market globalism* seeks to endow 'globalization' with free-market norms and neoliberal meanings. Contesting market globalism from the political Left, *justice globalism* constructs an alternative vision of globalization based on egalitarian ideals of global solidarity and distributive justice. From the political Right, various *religious globalisms* struggle against both market globalism and justice globalism as they seek to mobilize a religious community imagined in global terms in defence of religious values and beliefs that are thought to be under severe attack by the forces of secularism and consumerism.

In spite of their considerable differences, however, these three globalisms share nonetheless an important function: they articulate and translate the rising global imaginary—a background understanding of community and belonging increasingly tied to the global—into concrete political programmes and agendas. Hence, it would be inaccurate to accuse the two ideological challengers of dominant market globalism of being 'anti-globalization'. Rather, their position should be described as 'alter-globalization'—subscribing to alternative visions of an integrated world that resist neoliberal projections of universal free-market principles.

To be sure, *there are* powerful voices of 'anti-globalization'— national-populists and economic protectionists such as Donald Trump and most Tea Party adherents in the United States, Marine Le Pen in France, Nigel Farage in the UK, or Frauke Petry in Germany. Their respective programmes look very similar in their fierce opposition to globalizing dynamics that challenge national unity imagined in homogeneous terms.

In his successful 2016 US Presidential campaign, for example, Trump opposed the mainstream free trade stance of his party in favour of 'economic nationalism'—the view that the economy should be designed in ways that serve narrow national interests (see Illustration 15). Although his brand name 'Trump' stands for a *global* network of hotels from Honolulu to Rio de Janeiro, the

15. Donald Trump addressing a crowd in Milwaukee, Wis., 4 April 2016.

American entrepreneur and Reality TV host frequently expressed
his conviction that there exists at the core of contemporary
American society an irrepressible conflict between the claims of
American nationalism and the commands of the global economy.
Moreover, Trump advocated the building of a wall along the
1,989-mile border with Mexico to keep illegal immigrants out.
He also argued for the forcible deportation of millions of illegal
immigrants as well as a 'total and complete shutdown of
Muslims entering the United States until our country's [USA]
representatives can figure out what's going on'. Clinging to the
weakening national imaginary, national-populists like Trump can
be viewed as 'reactionaries' in the sense of reacting against all three
globalist ideologies without providing their national audiences
with constructive articulations of the rising global imaginary.

Market globalism

Market globalism is without question the dominant ideology of
our time. Since the 1990s, it has been codified and disseminated

worldwide by global power elites that include corporate managers, executives of large transnational corporations, corporate lobbyists, influential journalists and public-relations specialists, intellectuals writing for a large public audience, celebrities and top entertainers, state bureaucrats, and politicians. Serving as the chief advocates of market globalism, these individuals saturate the public discourse with idealized images of a consumerist, free-market world. Selling their preferred version of a single global marketplace to the public, they portray globalization in a positive light as an indispensable tool for the realization of such a global order.

Such favourable visions of globalization pervade public opinion and political choices in many parts of the world. Indeed, neoliberal decision-makers emerged as expert designers of an attractive ideological container for their market-friendly political agenda. Given that the exchange of commodities constitutes one of the core activities of all societies, the market-oriented discourse of globalization itself has turned into an extremely important commodity destined for public consumption. *Business Week*, *The Economist*, *Forbes*, the *Wall Street Journal*, and the *Financial Times* are among the most powerful of dozens of magazines, journals, newspapers, and electronic media published globally that feed their readers a steady diet of market-globalist claims.

Thus, market globalism has become what some social theorists call a 'strong discourse'—one that is notoriously difficult to resist and repel because it has on its side powerful social forces that have already pre-selected what counts as 'real' and, therefore, shape the world accordingly. The constant repetition and public recitation of market globalism's core claims and slogans have the capacity to produce what they name. As more neoliberal policies are enacted, the claims of market globalism become even more firmly planted in the public mind.

Analysing hundreds of newspaper and magazine articles—both online and offline—I have identified five major ideological claims

Box 8 The five claims of market globalism

1. Globalization is about the liberalization and global integration of markets
2. Globalization is inevitable and irreversible
3. Nobody is in charge of globalization
4. Globalization benefits everyone
5. Globalization furthers the spread of democracy in the world

that occur with great regularity in the utterances, speeches, and writings of influential market globalists (see Box 8).

It is important to note that globalists themselves construct these ideological claims in order to sell their political and economic agenda. Perhaps no single market-globalist speech or piece of writing contains all of the five assertions, but all of them contain at least some of these claims.

Like all ideologies, market globalism starts with the attempt to establish an authoritative definition of its core concepts. For neoliberals, such an account is anchored in the idea of the self-regulating market that serves as the framework for a future global order. But the problem with claim 1 is that its core message of liberalizing and integrating markets is only realizable through the *political* project of engineering free markets. Thus, market globalists must be prepared to utilize the *powers of government* to weaken and eliminate those social policies and institutions that curtail the market. Since only strong governments are up to this ambitious task of transforming existing social arrangements, the successful liberalization of markets depends upon *intervention* and *interference* by centralized state power. Such actions, however, stand in stark contrast to the neoliberal idealization of the limited role of government. Yet, globalists do expect governments to play an extremely active role in implementing their political agenda. The activist character of the earliest neoliberal administrations in the United States, the United Kingdom, Australia, and New Zealand during the 1980s and 1990s attests to the importance of strong governmental action in engineering free markets.

Claim 2 establishes the historical inevitability and irreversibility of globalization understood as the liberalization and global integration of markets. The portrayal of globalization as some sort of natural force, like the weather or gravity, makes it easier for market globalists to convince people that they must adapt to the discipline of the market if they are to survive and prosper. Hence, the claim of inevitability depoliticizes the public discourse about globalization. Neoliberal policies are portrayed to be above politics; they simply carry out what is ordained by nature. This implies that, instead of acting according to a set of choices, people merely fulfil world-market laws that demand the elimination of government controls. As former British Prime Minister Margaret Thatcher used to say, 'There is no alternative.' If nothing can be done about the natural movement of economic and technological forces, then political groups ought to acquiesce and make the best of an unalterable situation. Resistance would be unnatural, irrational, and dangerous.

Market globalism's deterministic language offers yet another rhetorical advantage. If the natural laws of the market have indeed preordained a neoliberal course of history, then globalization does not reflect the arbitrary agenda of a particular social class or group. In that case, market globalists merely carry out the unalterable imperatives of a transcendental force. People aren't in charge of globalization; markets and technology are. But those voices behind claim 3 are right only in a formal sense. While there is no conscious conspiracy orchestrated by a single, evil force, this does not mean that nobody is in charge of globalization. The liberalization and integration of global markets does not proceed outside the realm of human choice. As we will discuss in Chapter 8, the market-globalist initiative to integrate and deregulate markets around the world both creates and sustains asymmetrical power relations. Despite the rise of China and India, the United States is still the strongest economic and military power in the world, and the largest TNCs are based in North America. This is not to say that the USA rules supremely over these gigantic processes of globalization. But it *does* suggest that both the substance and the direction of globalization are to a significant degree shaped by American domestic and foreign policy.

Claim 4—globalization benefits everyone—lies at the very core of market globalism because it provides an affirmative answer to the crucial normative question of whether globalization should be considered a 'good' or a 'bad' thing. Market globalists frequently connect their arguments to the alleged benefits resulting from trade liberalization: rising global living standards, economic efficiency, individual freedom, and unprecedented technological progress. But when market dynamics dominate social and political outcomes, the opportunities and rewards of globalization are spread often unequally, concentrating power and wealth amongst a select group of people, regions, and corporations at the expense of the multitude. The same market logic also applies to access to information via digital technology (see Figure P). We will revisit the question of global inequality in Chapter 8.

Claim 5—globalization furthers the spread of democracy in the world—is rooted in the neoliberal assertion that free markets and democracy are synonymous terms. Persistently affirmed as 'common sense', the actual compatibility of these concepts often goes unchallenged in the public discourse. Indeed, claim 5 hinges on a conception of democracy that emphasizes formal procedures such as voting at the expense of the direct participation of broad majorities in political and economic decision-making. This 'thin' definition of democracy reflects an elitist and regimented model of 'low-intensity' or 'formal' market democracy. In practice, the crafting of a few democratic elements onto a basically authoritarian structure ensures that those elected remain

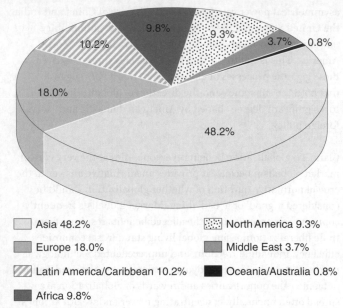

P. **Global Internet users by regions (2015).**

Source: Taken from <http://www.internetworldstats.com>, © 2015, Miniwatts Marketing Group

insulated from popular pressures and thus can govern 'effectively'. Hence, the assertion that globalization furthers the spread of democracy in the world is largely based on a superficial definition of democracy.

Our examination of the five central claims of market globalism suggests that the neoliberal language about globalization is ideological in the sense that it is politically motivated and contributes toward the construction of particular meanings of globalization that preserve and stabilize existing power relations. But the ideological reach of market globalism goes far beyond the task of providing the public with a narrow explanation of the meaning of globalization. Market globalism consists of powerful narratives that sell an overarching neoliberal worldview, thereby creating collective meanings and shaping people's identities. Yet, as both massive justice-globalist protests and jihadist-globalist acts of terrorism have shown, the expansion of market globalism has encountered considerable resistance from both progressives and traditionalists.

Justice globalism

As the 20th century was drawing to a close, criticisms of market globalism began to receive more attention in the public discourse on globalization, a development aided by a heightened awareness of how extreme corporate profit strategies were leading to widening global disparities in wealth and wellbeing. Starting in the late 1990s and continuing throughout much of the 2000s, the contest between market globalism and its ideological challenger on the political Left erupted in street confrontations in many cities around the world. Who are these justice-globalist forces and what is their ideological vision?

Justice globalism refers to the political ideas and values associated with the social alliances and political actors increasingly known as the 'global justice movement' (GJM). It emerged in the 1990s as a progressive network of international NGOs we defined in Chapter 4 as a 'global civil society'. Dedicated to the establishment of a more equitable relationship between the global North and South, the GJM agitated for the protection of the global environment, fair trade and international labour issues, human rights, and women's issues.

Challenging the central claims of market globalism, justice globalists believe that 'another world is possible', as one of their principal slogans suggests. Envisioning the construction of a new world order based on a global redistribution of wealth and power, the GJM emphasizes the crucial connection between globalization and local wellbeing. It accuses market-globalist elites of pushing neoliberal policies that are leading to greater global inequality, high levels of unemployment, environmental degradation, and the

Box 9 Global New Deal: five demands

1. A global 'Marshall Plan' that includes a blanket forgiveness of all Third World Debt;
2. Levying of the so-called 'Tobin Tax': a tax on international financial transactions that would benefit the global South;
3. Abolition of offshore financial centres that offer tax havens for wealthy individuals and corporations;
4. Implementation of stringent global environmental agreements;
5. Implementation of a more equitable global development agenda.

demise of social welfare. Calling for a 'Global New Deal' favouring the marginalized and poor, justice globalists seek to protect ordinary people all over the world from a neoliberal 'globalization from above' (see Box 9).

In North America, the progressive journalist Naomi Klein and the human rights proponent Noam Chomsky are leading representatives of justice globalism. In Europe, the spokespersons for established Green parties have long suggested that unfettered neoliberal globalization has resulted in a serious degradation of the global environment. Neo-anarchist groups in Europe and the United States such as the 'Black Bloc' concur with this perspective, and some of these groups are willing to make selective use of violent means in order to achieve their objectives. In the global South, justice globalism is often represented by democratic-popular and indigenous peoples' movements of resistance against neoliberal policies. Most of these groups have forged close links to other justice-globalist international NGOs (see Figure Q).

Today, there exist thousands of these organizations in all parts of the world. Some consist only of a handful of activists, while others attract a much larger membership.

Name of Organization	Location	Areas of concern/focus
Association pour une taxation des transactions financières pour l'aide aux citoyens (Association for the Taxation of Financial Transactions for the Aid of Citizens (ATTAC))	Paris, France plus multiple regional offices	Reform of global financial institutions and infrastructure
Articulación Feminista Mercosur (Southern Common Market)	Montevideo, Uruguay	Rights of women, indigenous people and the marginalized
Africa Trade Network	East Legion, Accra, Ghana	Trade and investment issues in Africa; reform of global financial system
Corpwatch	San Francisco, California, USA	Human, environmental, and worker rights at the local, national and global levels; transparency and accountability into global finance and trade
Food First International Action Network	Heidelberg, Germany	Promote the right to food, food sovereignty, and food security around the world
Focus on the Global South	Manila, Philippines; Bangkok, Thailand; Delhi, India	Policy research, advocacy, activism, and grassroots capacity building, critique of corporate-led globalization, neoliberalism and militarization

Q. Examples of justice-globalist organizations.

In the early 21st century, the forces of justice globalism have gathered political strength. This is evidenced by the emergence of the World Social Forum (WSF) and various 'Occupy' movements around the world. In the USA, Occupy Wall Street burst onto the political scene in 2011 as part of a global Occupy movement that drew activists in the world's major cities within months. Inspired by the popular protests of the 'Arab Spring' and Los Indignados ('the indigents') encampments in Spain, Occupy demonstrators expressed outrage at the inequalities of global capitalism and the irresponsible practices of many financial institutions, all of which had been on stark display during the Global Financial Crisis. Brandishing their slogan 'We are the 99%', Occupy protesters across the world occupied spaces of symbolic importance—such as New York City's Zuccotti Park near Wall Street—and sought to create—in miniature—the kind of egalitarian society they wanted to live in. Rejecting conventional organizational leadership formations, Occupy formed General Assemblies and working groups that reached decisions through a consensus-based process.

In spite of the mass appeal of the Occupy movement against the '1%', however, the WSF still serves as the key ideological site of justice globalism. It draws to its annual meetings in the global South tens of thousands of delegates from around the world. The proponents of justice globalism deliberately set up the WSF as a 'shadow organization' to the market-globalist World Economic Forum (WEF) in Davos, Switzerland. Just like market globalists who treat the WEF as a platform to project their ideas and values to a global audience, justice globalists utilize the WSF as the main production site of their ideological and policy alternatives (see Box 10).

Most of the justice-globalist groups affiliated with the WSF started out as small, seemingly insignificant groups of like-minded people in South America and Europe. Many of them learned important theoretical and practical lessons from justice-globalist struggles in developing countries, particularly from the Mexican

Box 10 From the WSF Charter of Principles

1. The World Social Forum is an open meeting place for reflective thinking, democratic debate of ideas, formulation of proposals, free exchange of experiences, and interlinking for effective action by groups and movements of civil society that are opposed to neoliberalism and to domination of the world by capital and any form of imperialism and are committed to building a planetary society directed toward fruitful relationships among humankind and between it and the Earth...

8. The World Social Forum is a plural, diversified, confessional, nongovernmental, and non-party context that, in a decentralized fashion, interrelates organizations and movements engaged in concrete action at levels from the local to the international to build another world...

13. As a context for interrelations, the World Social Forum seeks to strengthen and create new national and international links among organizations and movement of society that—in both public and private life—will increase the capacity for non-violent social resistance to the process of dehumanization the world is undergoing...

Zapatista Army of National Liberation 1994 uprising against neoliberal free trade policies (see Box 11).

Following five years later, the legendary 'Battle of Seattle' in late 1999 initiated a decade-long series of large-scale confrontations between the forces of market globalism and justice globalism. Taking part in this massive anti-WTO protest in Seattle, Washington, were 40,000 to 50,000 people. In spite of the predominance of North American participants, there was also a significant international presence. Articulating some of the five principal justice-globalist claims, this eclectic alliance included

Box 11 Five principal claims of justice globalism

1. Neoliberalism produces global crises.
2. Market-driven globalization has increased worldwide disparities in wealth and wellbeing.
3. Democratic participation is essential in solving global problems.
4. Another world is possible and urgently needed.
5. People power, not corporate power!

consumer activists, labour activists (including students demonstrating against sweatshops), environmentalists, animal rights activists, advocates of Third World debt relief, feminists, and human rights proponents. Eventually, large groups of demonstrators interrupted traffic in the city centre and managed to block off the main entrances to the convention centre by forming human chains. As hundreds of delegates were scrambling to make their way to the conference centre, Seattle police employed tear gas, batons, rubber bullets, and pepper spray stingers against the demonstrators (see Illustration 16). Altogether, the police arrested over 600 persons.

Ironically, the Battle of Seattle proved that many of the new technologies hailed by market globalists as the true hallmark of globalization could also be employed in the service of justice-globalist forces and their political agenda. Text messaging on mobile devices enabled the organizers of events like the one in Seattle to arrange for new forms of protest such as a series of demonstrations held simultaneously in various cities around the globe. As we have seen in the Middle East uprisings and the Occupy protests in the 2010s, individuals and groups all over the world can utilize social networking sites like Twitter and Facebook to readily and rapidly recruit new members, establish dates, share experiences, arrange logistics, and identify and publicize

16. Police confronting WTO protestors in downtown Seattle, 30 November 1999.

targets—activities that only two decades ago would have demanded much more time and money. Digital technologies also allow demonstrators not only to maintain close contact throughout the event, but also to react quickly and effectively to shifting police tactics. This enhanced ability to arrange and coordinate protests without the need for a central command, a clearly defined leadership, a large bureaucracy, and significant financial resources has added an entirely new dimension to the nature of justice-globalist demonstrations.

Religious globalisms

Justice globalists were preparing for a new wave of demonstrations against the IMF and World Bank, when Al Qaeda terrorists struck on 11 September 2001. Nearly 3,000 innocent people perished in less than two hours, including hundreds of heroic New York police and firefighters trapped in the collapsing towers of the World Trade Center (see Illustration 17). In the years following the attacks, it became clear that Islamist extremists were

123

17. The burning twin towers of the World Trade Center, 11 September 2001.

not confining their terrorist activities to the United States. Regional jihadist networks like ISIL, Al Qaeda, Jemaah Islamiya, Boko Haram, Al Shabaab, and Abu Sayyaf targeted civilians and military personnel around the globe, most recently in Paris (2015), Brussels (2016), Dhaka (2016), Istanbul (2016), and Nice (2016). In fact, jihadist globalists like Ahmed Omar, *emir* (leader) of the Somali jihadist network Al Shabaab, encourage Muslims residing in the West to organize their own independent terror cells in their 'holy war' against 'unbelief'—another chilling example of the intensifying 'glocalization' of human activities we discussed in Chapter 1.

But ISIL and Al Qaeda are but two extremely violent examples of organizations that subscribe to various forms of religious globalism. Other religiously inspired visions of global political community include some fundamentalist Christian groups such as the Army of God and Christian Identity, the Mormon Church, the Falun Gong sect, the Aum Shinrikyo cult, and Chabad, an orthodox Jewish movement with clear global ambitions. Despite their deep conservatism, religious globalisms also promote an alternative global vision. This is not to suggest that *all* religiously inspired visions of global community are conservative, reactionary, or violent. Indeed, most religions incorporate a sense of a global community united along religious lines, although in general this is largely informal. A key point about the religious globalist visions, however, is that these groups desire their version of a global religious community to be all-encompassing and to be given primacy and superiority over state-based and secular political structures. In some extreme cases like ISIL or Aum Shinrikyo, they are prepared to use extremely violent means to achieve their end goal.

While jihadist Islamism—represented by such groups as ISIL and Al Qaeda—is today's most spectacular manifestation of religious globalism, it would be a mistake to equate the ideology of the ISIL or Al Qaeda variety with the religion of Islam or even more peaceful strands of 'political Islam' or 'Islamist fundamentalism'. Rather, the term 'jihadist Islamism' is meant to apply to those extremely violent strains of Islam-influenced ideologies that articulate the global imaginary into concrete political agendas and terrorist strategies to be applied worldwide. As the recent terrorist activities of ISIL or Boko Haram have shown, jihadist Islamism is the most influential and successful attempt yet to articulate the rising global imaginary into a religious globalism—even after the killing of Osama bin Laden by US Navy SEALs in Pakistan on 2 May 2011 (see Box 12).

Jihadist Islamism is anchored in the core concepts of *umma* (Islamic community of believers) and *jihad* (armed or unarmed struggle against unbelief purely for the sake of God and his *umma*). Indeed, jihadist globalists understand the *umma* as a single community of believers united in their belief in the one and only God. Expressing a religious-populist yearning for strong leaders who set things right by fighting alien invaders and corrupt Islamic elites, they claim to return power back to the 'Muslim

Box 12 The late Osama bin Laden on *jihad* and the West

And the West's notion that Islam is a religion of *jihad* and enmity toward the religions of the infidels and the infidels themselves is an accurate and true depiction...For it is, in fact, part of our religion to impose our particular beliefs on others...Their [moderate Muslims] reluctance in acknowledging that offensive *jihad* is one of the exclusive traits of our religion demonstrates nothing but defeat. (2003)

I tell you [Americans] that the war [on terror] will be either ours or yours. If it is the former, it will mean your loss and your shame forever—and the winds are blowing in this direction, by Allah's grace. But if it is the latter, then read history, for we are a people who do not stand for injustice, and we strive for vengeance all days of our lives. And the days and nights will not pass until we avenge ourselves as we did on September 11. (2006)

masses' and restore the *umma* to its earlier glory. In their view, the process of regeneration must start with a small but dedicated vanguard of warriors willing to sacrifice their lives as martyrs to the holy cause of awakening people to their religious duties—not just in traditionally Islamic countries, but wherever members of the *umma* yearn for the establishment of God's rule on earth. With a third of the world's Muslims living today as minorities in non-Islamic countries, jihadist Islamists regard the restoration as no longer a local, national, or even regional event. Rather, it requires a concerted *global* effort spearheaded by jihadists operating in various localities around the world.

Thus, jihadist globalism takes place in a global space emancipated from the confining territoriality of 'Egypt', or the 'Middle East' that used to constitute the political framework of religious nationalists fighting modern secular regimes in the 20th century. Although organizations like ISIL embrace the Manichean dualism of a 'clash of civilizations' between their imagined *umma* and 'global unbelief', their globalist ideology clearly transcends clear-cut civilizational fault lines. Their desire for the restoration of a transnational *umma* attests to the globalization of the Muslim world just as much as it reflects the Islamization of the West. Constructed in the ideational transition from the national to the global imaginary, jihadist Islamism still retains potent metaphors that resonate with people's national or even tribal solidarities. And yet, their focus is firmly on the global as jihadist Islamists have successfully redirected militant Islamism's struggle from the traditional 'Near Enemy' (secular-nationalist Middle Eastern regimes) to the 'Far Enemy' (the globalizing West).

Jihadist globalism's core ideological claim—to rebuild a unified global *umma* through global *jihad* against global unbelief—resonates well with the dynamics of a globalizing world. It holds special appeal for Muslim youths between the ages of 15 and 30 who have lived for sustained periods of time in the individualized and deculturated environments of Westernized Islam. This new wave of jihadist recruits, responsible for the most spectacular terrorist operations like the Brussels bombings of 22 March 2016, were products of a Westernized Islam. Most of them resided in Europe or North Africa and had few or no links to traditional Middle East political parties. Their enthusiasm for the establishment of a transnational *umma* by means of *jihad* made them prime candidates for recruitment. These young men followed in the footsteps of Al Qaeda's 'first-wavers' in Afghanistan in the 1980s who developed their ideological outlook among a multinational band of idealistic *mujahideen* bent on bringing down the 'godless' Soviet empire.

Their extremist rhetoric notwithstanding, jihadist Islamists never lose sight of the fact that jihadist globalists are fighting a steep uphill battle against the secular forces of market globalism and justice globalism. And yet, even against seemingly overwhelming military odds that translated into a significant weakening of the Al Qaeda network over the last decade, new powerful jihadist organizations like ISIL have emerged in recent years. Taking advantage of the shifting power dynamics in the Islamic world, ISIL leaders have been able to recruit as many as 30,000 foreigners to their principal battlegrounds in Syria, Iraq, and Libya in the 2010s. Despite its chilling and violent content, their vision contains an ideological alternative to market globalism and justice globalism that nonetheless imagines community in unambiguously global terms.

Chapter 8
The future of globalization

In the two decades following 9/11, the ideological struggle over the meaning and direction of globalization has shown no signs of dissipating. In fact, the election of the national populist business tycoon Donald Trump to the world's most powerful political office has cast a long shadow over the future prospects for international cooperation. After all, the intensification of social relations across world-space and world-time has both generated and responded to new global problems that are beyond the reach of any single nation-state. Perhaps the three most daunting tasks facing humanity in the 21st century are the reduction of global inequality, the preservation of our wondrous planet, and the strengthening of human security. The growing disparities in wealth and wellbeing, in particular, cast a dark shadow on the final question we will consider in this very short introduction to globalization: will we tackle our global problems in a cooperative manner or are we on the brink of a new era of conflict that might halt the powerful momentum of globalization?

On first thought, it is obvious that even such protracted global crises as the Global Financial Crisis could not stop such a powerful set of social processes as globalization. In fact, the emergence of the Group of Twenty (G20) as a rather effective deliberative body with the ability to design and coordinate action on a global scale suggests that the idea of global governance is perhaps not as utopian today as it was only a quarter-century ago. Other success stories such as the worldwide reduction of absolute poverty and the formation of an international alliance dedicated to the joint exploration of outer space suggest that the solution to our global problems is not less but more (and better forms of) globalization. On the other hand, there is no dearth of political and cultural conflicts such as the new expansionist policies of Russian President Putin in Eastern Europe and the Caucasus region, the aggressive nuclear stance of North Korean Supreme Leader Kim Jong Un, the failed 2016 coup in Turkey and President Erdogan's imposed state of emergency, and the murderous terrorist attacks of religious globalist organizations like ISIL that exploded in number and intensity in 2016. Indeed, a close look at modern history reveals that large and lasting social crises often lead to the rise of extremist political groups. The large-scale violence they unleashed proved capable of stopping and even reversing previous globalization trends.

As we noted in Chapter 2, the period from 1860 to 1914 constituted such an earlier phase of globalization, characterized by the expansion of transportation and communication networks, the rapid growth of international trade, and a huge flow of capital. Great Britain, then the most dominant of the world's 'Great Powers', sought to spread its political system and cultural values across the globe in much the same way the United States does today. But this earlier period of globalization was openly imperialistic in character, involving the forced transfer of resources from the colonized global South in exchange for European manufactures. Liberalism, Great Britain's chief ideology, translated a national, not a global, imaginary into concrete political programmes that benefited the Empire at the expense of its colonies. In the end, these sustained efforts to maintain British political and economic hegemony contributed to a severe backlash in the form of a frantic European arms race that culminated in the outbreak of the Great War in 1914.

In an enduring study on this subject, the insightful Austrian political economist Karl Polanyi located the origins of the social crises that gripped the world during the first half of the 20th century in ill-conceived efforts to liberalize and globalize markets. Commercial interests came to dominate society by means of a ruthless market logic that effectively disconnected people's economic activities from their social relations. The competitive rules of the free market destroyed complex social relations of mutual obligation and undermined deep-seated norms and values such as civic engagement, reciprocity, and redistribution. As large segments of the population found themselves without an adequate system of social security and communal support, they resorted to radical measures to protect themselves against the globalization of minimally regulated markets.

Polanyi noted that these European movements against unfettered capitalism eventually gave birth to political parties that forced the passage of protective social legislation on the national level. After a prolonged period of severe economic dislocation following the end of the Great War, such national-protectionist impulses experienced their most extreme manifestations in Italian fascism and German Nazism. In the end, the liberal dream of subordinating all nation-states to the requirements of the free market had generated an equally extreme counter-movement that turned markets into mere appendices of the totalitarian state.

The applicability of Polanyi's analysis to the current situation seems obvious. Like its 19th-century predecessor, today's globalization of markets also represents a gigantic experiment in unleashing economic deregulation and a culture of consumerism on the entire world. Like 19th-century Britain, the United States is the dominant cheerleader of neoliberalism and thus draws both admiration and contempt from less developed regions in the world. But it appears that America's status as the world's 'hyperpower' might not endure indefinitely. China, India, Russia, and other so-called 'Rising Powers' will force the USA to share the responsibility of global leadership.

Still, those who find themselves to be disadvantaged and exploited by a global logic of economic integration tend to blame 'international elites'. Thus, we have already been confronted with previously unthinkable forms of nationalist backlash like Brexit in the UK, the Trump presidency in the US, and the rise of other extremist populists around the world who blame rising levels of inequality and insecurity on 'globalization'. Most political pundits still underestimate the power of this populist anti-globalization message—even after the stunning 2016 election victory of Trump in the home country of neoliberalism. Drawing a sharp line between 'us' and 'them', national populists like Donald Trump, Marine Le Pen, and Nigel Farage successfully convinced large sectors of their electorate that supporting 'globalists' was tantamount to handing control of 'their' country over to immigrants, terrorists, economic elites, and faceless bureaucrats operating in central government structures.

The search for more inclusive ways of dealing with global problems must eschew national populism and instead draw on a more cosmopolitan spirit that calls for the creation of new global institutions and cooperative networks. Only a decade ago, in the wake of the first powerful justice-globalist demonstrations, representatives of the wealthy countries assured audiences worldwide that they would be willing to reform the global economic architecture in the direction of greater transparency and accountability. Unfortunately, little progress has been made to honour these commitments and reverse the conditions of economic and political inequality that remain at the centre of many related global problems.

Indeed, in recent years, there has been a growing chorus of commentators from a variety of ideological perspectives who have pointed to the growing gap between the rich and poor that also includes a growing digital divide separating countries in the global North and South. In his path-breaking study on the long-term historical changes in the concentration of income and wealth, the French economist Thomas Piketty argues that today's levels of social inequality in most countries are approaching those shocking disparities that existed throughout the 19th century. In the United States, for example, income inequality in the 2010s has returned to the troubling extremes that were last seen at the height of the Roaring Twenties in 1928–9. Thus, Piketty recommends the adoption of a global tax on wealth to prevent soaring inequality from feeding once again the monster of economic and political instability in the world.

Still, as the 'big data' recently collected by Branko Milanovic reveal, there are also some encouraging trends related to income equality among the citizens of the world. In particular, the prominent Serbian-American economist documents the rise of what might be called a 'global middle class', most of whom are located in China and the other parts of the emerging Asian region. On the downside, however, Milanovic confirms Piketty's observations of the stagnation of lower middle-class groups in the rich world that are still globally well off but are losing ground nationally. Finally, he presents strong evidence for the growth of a 'global plutocracy'—a tiny group of super-wealthy, interconnected elites that exert tremendous political and social influence around the world (see Figure R). The strengthening of such patterns of inequality does not bode well for the prospects of democracy in the globalizing world of the 21st century.

Without question, the years and decades ahead will bring new global crises and further challenges. Humanity has reached yet another critical juncture—the most important in the relatively short existence of our species. Unless we are willing to let global problems fester to the point where violence and intolerance appear to be the only realistic ways of confronting our unevenly integrating world, we must link the future course of globalization

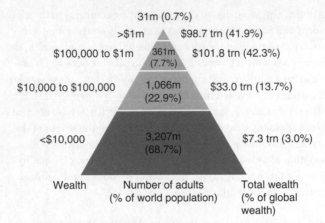

R. Global wealth distribution (2015).

Source: Statista

to a profoundly reformist agenda. As I emphasized in the
Preface of this book, we ought to reject the siren call of national
populists and instead welcome greater manifestations of social
interdependence that emerge as a result of globalization. These
transformative social processes must be guided by the ethical
polestar of cosmopolitanism: the building of a truly democratic
and egalitarian global order that protects universal human rights
without destroying the cultural diversity that is the lifeblood of
human evolution.

References

There is a great deal of academic literature on globalization. But many of these books are not easily accessible to those who are just setting out to acquire some knowledge of the subject. However, readers who have already digested the present volume may find it easier to approach some of the academic works listed at the end of the book. While these works do not exhaust the long list of publications on the subject, they nonetheless represent what I consider to be the most appropriate sources for further reading. Indeed, some of them have influenced the arguments made in the present volume. Following the overall organization of this book series, however, I have kept direct quotations to a minimum. Still, I wish to acknowledge my intellectual debt to these authors, whose influence on this book is not always obvious from the text.

Chapter 1: Globalization: a contested concept

Accessible academic books and texts on globalization published in recent years include: Jan Aart Scholte, *Globalization*, 2nd edn (St Martin's Press, 2005); Saskia Sassen, *A Sociology of Globalization* (Norton, 2007); Manfred B. Steger, *Globalisms: The Great Ideological Struggle of the 21st Century* (Rowman & Littlefield, 2009); and George Ritzer and Paul Dean, *Globalization: A Basic Text*, 2nd edn (Wiley-Blackwell, 2015).
For representative collections of influential essays and excerpts on globalization, see George Ritzer (ed.), *The Blackwell Companion to Globalization* (Blackwell, 2007); Manfred B. Steger, Paul

Battersby, and Joseph Siracusa (eds), *The SAGE Handbook of Globalization*, 2 vols (Sage Publications, 2014); and Frank J. Lechner and John Boli (eds), *The Globalization Reader*, 5th edn (Wiley Blackwell, 2015). Manuel Castells's *Communication Power* (Oxford University Press, 2011) maps the contours of today's 'global network society'. A comprehensive elucidation of leading theoretical approaches to understanding globalization can be found in Barrie Axford, *Theories of Globalization* (Polity, 2014).

There are now several excellent academic journals dedicated to the study of globalization. Some of the most influential include: *Globalizations*, *Global Networks*, *New Global Studies*, and *Journal of Critical Globalisation Studies*.

For an introduction to the transdisciplinary field of global studies, see Manfred B. Steger and Amentahru Wahlrab, *What Is Global Studies? Theory & Practice* (Routledge, 2017).

Information on the 2014 World Cup used in this chapter can be gleaned from the following Internet source: <http://www.fifa.com/worldcup/archive/brazil2014>.

The parable of the blind scholars and the elephant most likely originated in the Pali Buddhist Udana, a collection of Buddhist stories compiled in the 2nd century BCE. The many versions of the parable spread to other religions as well, especially to Hinduism and Islam. My thanks go to Professor Ramdas Lamb at the University of Hawai'i at Mānoa for sharing his understanding of the story.

Chapter 2: Globalization in history: is globalization a new phenomenon?

My discussion in the early part of this chapter has greatly benefited from the arguments made by Jared Diamond in his Pulitzer-prize-winning book *Guns, Germs, and Steel* (Norton, 1999). I also recommend a delightful and very readable history of globalization assembled by Nayan Chandra, *Bound Together: How Traders, Preachers, Adventurers, and Warriors Shaped Globalization* (Yale University Press, 2007).

Some of the essential books surveying the growing field of global history include: Bruce Mazlish, *The New Global History* (Routledge, 2006); Pamela Kyle Crossley, *What is Global History?* (Polity, 2008); Jürgen Osterhammel and Niels P. Petersson,

Globalization: A Short History (Princeton University Press, 2009);
Dominic Sachsenmeier, *Global Perspectives on Global History:
Theories and Approaches to a Connected World* (Cambridge
University Press, 2011); and Sebastian Conrad, *What Is Global
History?* (Princeton University Press, 2016). Two excellent
academic journals on the subject are: *Journal of World History*
and *Journal of Global History.*

An accessible account of 'world-system theory' authored by Immanuel
Wallerstein can be found in his *World-System Analysis: An
Introduction* (Duke University Press, 2004).

Chapter 3: The economic dimension of globalization

Accessible treatments of economic globalization are provided by
Joseph Stiglitz, *Making Globalization Work* (W. W. Norton,
2007); Pietra Rivoli, *The Travels of a T-Shirt in the Global
Economy*, 2nd edn (Wiley, 2015); and Peter Dicken, *Global Shift:
Mapping the Contours of the World Economy*, 7th edn (The
Guilford Press, 2015).

An overview of neoliberalism can be found in Manfred B. Steger and
Ravi K. Roy, *Neoliberalism: A Very Short Introduction* (Oxford
University Press, 2010).

The best short treatment of the Global Financial Crisis is Robert J.
Holton, *Global Finance* (Routledge, 2012). A readable insider
account of the GFC's origins and evolution can be found in Joseph
E. Stiglitz, *Freefall: America, Free Markets, and the Sinking of the
World Economy* (Norton, 2010).

My short summary of the Greek Debt Crisis has benefited from
the *New York Times* article 'Greece's Debt Crisis Explained',
International Business Editorial (9 November 2015):
<http://www.nytimes.com/interactive/2015/business/
international/greece-debt-crisis-euro.html>. A short overview of
the impact of the Chinese economic slowdown can be found in
Chris Giles, 'World Economy Feels the Impact when China takes a
Knock', *Financial Times* (7 January 2016): <https://www.ft.com/
content/30441208-b548-11e5-b147-e5e5bba42e51>.

The findings of the groundbreaking study of TNC networks referred to
in this chapter can be found in Stefania Vitali, James B. Glattfelder,
and Stefano Battiston, 'The Network of Global Corporate Control',
PLoS One 6.10 (October 2011), pp. 1–6.

References

The best sources for empirical data on economic globalization are the annual editions of the UN *Human Development Report* (Oxford University Press), the World Bank's *World Development Report* (Oxford University Press), and the WTO's annual *International Trade Statistics*.

Chapter 4: The political dimension of globalization

An accessible description of the Westphalian model is offered by David Held, Anthony McGrew, David Goldblatt, and Jonathan Perraton, *Global Transformations* (Stanford University Press, 1999), pp. 37–8. My own discussion of political globalization has greatly benefited from insights contained in chapter 1 of this study. Another excellent introduction to political globalization is John Baylis and Steve Smith, *The Globalization of World Politics*, 6th edn (Oxford University Press, 2014).

For the arguments of globalizers, see Martin Wolf, *Why Globalization Works* (Yale University Press, 2005); and Kenichi Ohmae, *The End of the Nation-State* (Free Press, 1995). For the position of the globalization sceptics, see John Ralston Saul, *The Collapse of Globalism* (Viking, 2005); and Peter Gowan, *The Global Gamble* (Verso, 1999). Saskia Sassen's important work on territoriality and global cities contains both sceptical and globalist arguments. See, for example, *Territory, Authority, Rights: From Medieval to Global Assemblages* (Princeton University Press, 2008), and *The Global City: New York, London, Tokyo*, 2nd edn (Princeton University Press, 2001).

On the topic of global politics, economics, public policy, and governance, see James H. Mittelman, *Hyperconflict: Globalization and Insecurity* (Stanford University Press, 2010); Jan Aart Scholte, *Building Global Democracy: Civil Society and Accountable Global Governance* (Cambridge University Press, 2011); and Thomas G. Weiss, *Global Governance: Why What Whither* (Polity Press, 2013).

For the full report issued by MSF/DWB on the 2013–16 Ebola epidemic, see <http://www.doctorswithoutborders.org/our-work/medical-issues/ebola>.

David Held's elements of cosmopolitan democracy are taken from Daniele Archibugi and David Held (eds), *Cosmopolitan Democracy* (Polity Press, 1995), pp. 96–120.

Chapter 5: The cultural dimension of globalization

For a comprehensive study on the cultural dimensions of globalization, see Jan Nederveen Pieterse, *Globalization and Culture: Global Melange*, 3rd edn (Rowman and Littlefield, 2015).

For the arguments of pessimistic globalizers, see Benjamin Barber, *Consumed* (W. W. Norton and Company, 2007). For the arguments of optimistic globalizers, see Thomas L. Friedman, *The World Is Flat 3.0: A Brief History of the Twenty-First Century* (Picador, 2007). For the arguments of the sceptics, see Arjun Appadurai, *Modernity at Large* (University of Minnesota Press, 1996); and Roland Robertson, *Globalization* (Sage, 1992).

For the pivotal role of the global media, see Jack Lule, *Globalization and the Media: Global Village of Babel*, 2nd edn (Rowman & Littlefield, 2015).

On English as a global language, see Robert McCrum, *Globish: How the English Language Became the World's Language* (W. W. Norton, 2010).

Chapter 6: The ecological dimension of globalization

An accessible yet remarkably comprehensive book on ecological globalization is Peter Christoff and Robyn Eckersley, *Globalization and the Environment* (Rowman & Littlefield, 2013). My arguments in this chapter have greatly benefited from the authors' insights presented in their learned study.

For a concise introduction to global climate change issues that also effectively debunks the myths of climate change deniers, see Joseph Romm, *Climate Change: What Everyone Needs to Know* (Oxford University Press, 2016).

For a short but comprehensive summary of the effects of global climate change, see Melissa Denchak, 'Are the Effects of Global Warming Really that Bad?' (15 March 2016), <https://www.nrdc.org/stories/are-effects-global-warming-really-bad>.

For the Stern Report, see Nicholas Stern, *The Economics of Climate Change: The Stern Review* (Cambridge University Press, 2007).

The 5th edition of the UN Environment Program's *Global Environmental Outlook* (2012) can be found at: <http://www.unep.org/climatechange/>. The 6th edition is expected to be launched in late 2017.

The full text of Pope Francis's *Laudato Si* can be found at: <http://w2.vatican.va/content/francesco/en/encyclicals/documents/papa-francesco_20150524_enciclica-laudato-si.html>.

For a short summary of the Paris Climate Agreement, see Helen Briggs, 'Global Climate Deal: In Summary', BBC News, <http://www.bbc.com/news/science-environment-35073297>.

Chapter 7: Ideologies of globalization: market globalism, justice globalism, religious globalisms

For a more detailed account of the ideological dimensions of globalization, see Manfred B. Steger, *The Rise of the Global Imaginary: Political Ideologies from the French Revolution to the Global War on Terror* (Oxford University Press, 2009); and *Globalisms: The Great Ideological Struggle of the 21st Century*, 3rd edn (Rowman & Littlefield, 2009).

Readable accounts of globalization from a market-globalist perspective include: Jagdish Bhagwati, *In Defense of Globalization* (Oxford University Press, 2007); and Daniel Cohen, *Globalization and its Enemies* (MIT Press, 2007).

The justice-globalist claims and information on global justice movement in general can be found in: Manfred B. Steger, James Goodman, and Erin K. Wilson, *Justice Globalism: Ideology, Crises, Policy* (Sage, 2013); and Geoffrey Pleyers, *Alter-Globalization: Becoming Actors in the Global Age* (Polity, 2010).

An accessible introduction to the evolution and ideas of the US Occupy movement is provided by Nicholas Smaligo, *The Occupy Movement Explained* (Open Court, 2014).

For an insightful discussion of the impact of globalization on Islam, see Nevzat Soguk, *Globalization and Islamism: Beyond Fundamentalism* (Rowman & Littlefield, 2011). Two excellent academic treatments of jihadist globalism and its affiliated movements can be found in: Olivier Roy, *Globalized Islam: The Search for the New Ummah* (Columbia University Press, 2006); and Roel Meijer, *Global Salafism: Islam's New Religious Movement* (Oxford University Press, 2014).

The excerpts from Osama bin Laden's speeches and writings are taken from Raymond Ibrahim (ed.), *The Al Qaeda Reader* (Broadway Books, 2007); and Bruce Lawrence (ed.), *Messages to the World: The Statements of Osama bin Laden* (Verso, 2005).

Chapter 8: The future of globalization

For the classic discussion of the backlash against globalization in the interwar period, see Karl Polanyi, *The Great Transformation* (Beacon Press, 2001 [1944]).

On the subject of global inequality, see Thomas Piketty, *Capital in the Twenty-First Century* (The Belknap Press, 2014); Branko Milanovic, *Global Inequality: A New Approach for the Age of Globalization* (The Belknap Press, 2016); and Robert J. Holton, *Global Inequalities* (Palgrave Macmillan, 2014).

Index

Globalization